Corrective Mathematics

Series Guide

A Direct Instruction Program

M000094062

Siegfried Engelmann • Doug Carnine • Don Steely

Columbus, OH

The **McGraw·Hill** Companies

SRAonline.com

Contents

Introduction to Corrective Mathematics

Corrective Mathematics is a series of seven modules intended as an intervention program for students grade 3 through adult. The modules include

- Addition
- Subtraction
- Multiplication
- Division
- Basic Fractions
- Fractions, Decimals, and Percents
- Ratios and Equations

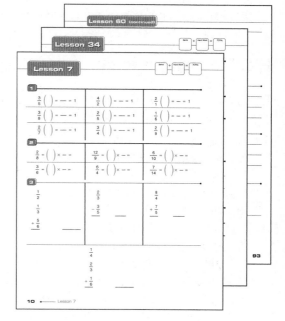

The series focuses on core concepts, rules, and mathematical reasoning to help students

- learn and retain facts.
- understand place value.
- understand fractions, decimals, and percents.
- solve computational problems.
- accurately translate word problems into numerical statements.

Corrective Mathematics is designed to provide strategic and intensive instruction to students grade 3 through adult who have difficulty achieving at grade level. By focusing on core content and breaking this content into a series of small conceptual steps and embedded skills, the series helps these struggling students learn efficiently from grade-level instructional materials.

Corrective Mathematics is organized by modules.

- The modular approach makes the series flexible so it can be applied to a wide variety of learning situations.
- The Comprehensive Placement Test provides a plan that identifies which modules need to be covered.
- The series is not intended to serve as a fixed course of study. Instead, it is used to support a high-quality core mathematics program.

Corrective Mathematics enables you to
teach mathematics skills, rules, and strategies efficiently and effectively. It ensures that students will learn to work mathematic problems accurately and confidently.

Corrective Mathematics can be presented
to large groups, but students are best served when in groups of 15 or fewer. The modules can also be used with individual students in resource-room settings.

If a module is being taught to several groups of students, the students should be grouped homogeneously on the basis of their scores on the placement test.

Components for each module of *Corrective Mathematics* include:

- Teacher's Presentation Book
- Workbook
- Answer Key
- **Exam***View*® software (available separately)

2005 Edition

The 2005 edition of *Corrective Mathematics* contains significant improvements over earlier editions.

- Scripting in the Teacher Presentation Books has been revised to the newer Direct Instruction styles, making lessons easier to use.
- New design features allow you to preview, present, and review lessons more efficiently.
- Facts-Practice Blackline Masters have been added to the *Addition, Subtraction, Multiplication,* and *Division* modules to help students become fluent with math facts.
- Reproducible Cumulative Review Worksheets in the *Subtraction, Multiplication,* and *Division* modules boost student proficiency of previously learned operations.

New Software

The new software program, **Exam***View*® for *Corrective Mathematics,* provides dynamic worksheets for each module of *Corrective Mathematics* and lets you create your own paper- or computer-based tests and worksheets.

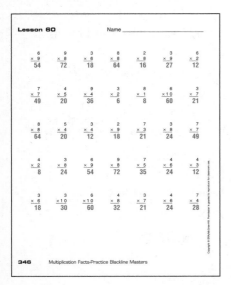

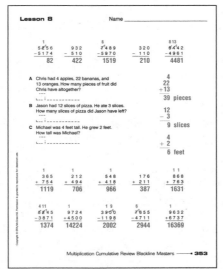

Materials for Each Module

- Teacher Presentation Book
  - ◆ Guide section contains information for presenting exercises, correcting mistakes, and administering the preskill and placement tests
  - ◆ Presentation section contains detailed lesson plans
- Answer Key
- Workbook
  - ◆ Daily worksheets and point summary chart for recording student performance and awarding grades
- **Exam***View*® software (available separately)

Addition

Organization	Content
• 65 lessons • 25–45 minutes per lesson • 14 in-program mastery tests • 27 Facts-Practice Blackline Masters	• 100 basic addition facts • operation of addition • reading and writing numbers into the thousands • column addition with 3- and 4-digit numbers • addition with carrying • story problems with distracters

Subtraction

Organization	Content
• 65 lessons • 25–45 minutes per lesson • 18 in-program mastery tests • 29 Facts-Practice Blackline Masters • 32 Cumulative Review Blackline Masters	• 100 basic subtraction facts • operation of subtraction • renaming (borrowing) • reading and writing numbers into the thousands • subtraction story problems • story problems that require discrimination between addition and subtraction

Multiplication

Organization	Content
• 65 lessons • 25–45 minutes per lesson • 15 in-program mastery tests • 29 Facts-Practice Blackline Masters • 32 Cumulative Review Blackline Masters	• 100 basic multiplication facts • operation of multiplication • reading and writing thousands numbers • multiplication story problems • story problems that require discrimination among multiplication, addition, and subtraction

Division

Organization	Content
• 65 lessons • 25–45 minutes per lesson • 16 in-program mastery tests • Facts-Practice Blackline Masters • Cumulative Review Blackline Masters	• 100 basic division facts • the long division operation (with either 1- or 2-digit divisors) • story problems that require the division operation • division story problems • procedures for discriminating between division story problems and story problems that require addition, subtraction, or multiplication

Basic Fractions

Organization	Content
• 55 lessons • 20 minutes per lesson • 7 review worksheets	• write fractions from pictures • draw pictures from fractions • determine when a fraction is equal to 1, more than 1, and less than 1 • add and subtract fractions with a common denominator • change whole numbers and mixed numbers to fractions • add, subtract, and multiply fractions and mixed numbers

Fractions, Decimals, and Percents

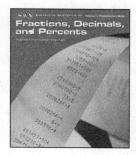

Organization	Content
• 70 lessons + 3 review lessons • 30 minutes per lesson	• add and subtract fractions with unlike denominators • reduce improper fractions • multiply and divide fractions • find equivalent fractions • find the largest in a series of fractions • write decimals as fractions • use decimal notation • add, subtract, multiply, and divide decimal numbers • rewrite mixed fractions as mixed decimals • convert fractions to decimals to percents

Ratios and Equations

Organization	Content
• 60 lessons • 25 minutes per lesson	• basic ratio analysis • ratio word problems

Major skills and concepts are detailed on the Scope and Sequence charts beginning on page 13 of this guide.

Overview of Skill Development

Each module has four groups of activities that occur from one lesson to the next. These are called tracks. Each module has four different tracks: Facts, Place Value, Operations, and Story Problems.

Facts Track

The fact activities are designed to promote instructional economy and a high level of student proficiency. Instructional economy is ensured because the modules do not treat each fact as a separate entity to be memorized, but rather as a member of both a number family and a fact series.

Number families consist of three numbers that go together to form a basic fact. In the *Addition* module, students work with number families that look like this:

$$\boxed{5} \begin{cases} 4 \\ \\ 1 \end{cases}$$

The number in the box is referred to as the "big number." The numbers inside the bracket are referred to as the "small numbers." The students learn that "the big number is the number you end up with when you add the two small numbers." Learning number families is instructionally economical because each number family translates into two addition facts. The number family above, for instance, translates into $4 + 1 = 5$ and $1 + 4 = 5$.

$$\boxed{5} \begin{cases} 4 \quad \cdots 4 + 1 = 5 \cdots \\ \\ 1 \quad \cdots 1 + 4 = 5 \cdots \end{cases}$$

The *Subtraction* module uses the same number families as the *Addition* module. Learning the subtraction facts, therefore, involves a variation of something familiar. This is doubly efficient learning. In the *Subtraction* module, students learn that "there are two subtraction facts for each number family. Subtraction facts always start with the big number." At this point, the students use the number family 5, 4, 1 to generate four facts:
$4 + 1 = 5, 1 + 4 = 5, 5 - 4 = 1,$
and $5 - 1 = 4$.

A different type of number family is used in the *Multiplication* module. The multiplication number family is shown in the shape of a division problem.

This distinguishes multiplication facts from addition and subtraction facts, and it will promote the relationship between multiplication and division. The students learn that the number in the box is the "big number" and the numbers outside the bracket are the "small numbers." They also learn that "when you multiply the two small numbers, you end up with the big number." The number family 3, 5, 15 becomes
$5 \times 3 = 15$ and $3 \times 5 = 15$.

The *Division* module makes use of the number families taught in *Multiplication,* so once again, the fact learning is doubly efficient. The students learn that "when you write the division sign, the big number goes under the sign. One small number goes before the sign. The other small number goes above the last digit of the big number."

$$3\overline{)15}^{\,5}$$

The number family 3, 5, 15 becomes $5 \times 3 = 15$, $3 \times 5 = 15$, $3\overline{)15}^{\,5}$, and $5\overline{)15}^{\,3}$.

Another way in which *Corrective Mathematics* shows the relationship among various facts is through **fact series** exercises. Facts are presented in order, to show their relationship to counting. For example, in the series $6 + 1 = 7$, $6 + 2 = 8$, and $6 + 3 = 9$, every time a number is counted in the second addend (1, 2, 3), the number is counted in the sum (7, 8, 9). By teaching fact relationships, individual facts are easier to master and recall. Here are sample fact series from each of the four modules:

Addition $10 + 1 = 11$

$10 + 2 = 12$
$10 + 3 = 13$
$10 + 4 = 14$
$10 + 5 = 15$

Subtraction $15 - 10 = 5$

$14 - 10 = 4$
$13 - 10 = 3$
$12 - 10 = 2$
$11 - 10 = 1$

Multiplication $5 \times 1 = 5$

$5 \times 2 = 10$
$5 \times 3 = 15$
$5 \times 4 = 20$
$5 \times 5 = 25$

Division

$6\overline{)36}^{\,6}$

$6\overline{)42}^{\,7}$

$6\overline{)48}^{\,8}$

$6\overline{)54}^{\,9}$

$6\overline{)60}^{\,10}$

Facts Practice

Once the students have a number of firm reference points and know how to use these reference points to figure out closely related facts, the modules provide a number of exercises designed to increase student proficiency with individual facts. Students work with facts in a variety of teacher-directed and independent activities, both oral and written.

Two of the most enjoyable of these activities are the **Fact Game,** in which groups of students compete, and the **Timing Format,** in which individual students earn points for speed and accuracy on fact worksheets. The Fact Game is an extremely important way of providing students with the practice they need to master facts. Because drill and practice can be boring to students, you need to reinforce student improvement and use games or challenges to motivate students.

The speed requirements specified in the modules are quite low. Whenever possible, require students to increase the rate at which they work fact exercises. If students cannot answer 40 facts per minute at the end of a module, continue drilling those facts even though students have completed the module.

Also, Facts-Practice Blackline Masters are provided in each of the four operations modules for optional facts practice. These may be used anytime during the day.

Cumulative review blackline masters are provided for *Subtraction, Multiplication,* and *Division.*

Fact Mastery Tests

In addition to providing the amount of practice students need to become proficient on facts, the four modules also provide a vehicle for monitoring student proficiency. Fact Mastery Tests appear frequently in each of the modules. Students are tested for speed and accuracy. Instructions that accompany the tests provide criteria for evaluating test scores and remediation for students who fail.

Special Facts

Corrective Mathematics also teaches fact relationships usually omitted in other instructional programs. Division facts are taught in most programs, but division remainder facts are not. For example, students are taught

$$5 \overline{)30}^{\,6}$$

but are not taught that 5 goes into 31, 32, 33, and 34, 6 times. *Corrective Mathematics* devotes a great deal of time to division remainder facts.

Another example from *Corrective Mathematics* is the way in which problems such as 18 + 8 = 26 are taught. Students learn to silently compute the answer to this type of problem. Teaching these problems as "facts" aids in the solution of many addition and multiplication problems such as the following:

```
         8
    18          29          59⟩  18
  +  8        ×  9          19⟩
  ————        ————        + 28⟩
    26         26①          ————
                            10⑥
```

Operations Track

Each module teaches a coherent problem-solving routine that allows students to handle a wide variety of computational problems. The routines provide for all subtypes of problems that students might encounter, such as borrowing from zero in subtraction and multiplying by a number with a zero in the ones column.

Addition

The addition operation is taught in stages. First, the students add columns of single-digit numbers. Then, they are taught to add columns of numbers that have more than one digit but that do not require renaming (carrying). When carrying is introduced, the sum for the ones column is given, and the students write only the number being carried in a box at the top of the tens column. Later, the sum is no longer written, and then, the carrying box is dropped. The operation is expanded so that carrying occurs not only from the ones column but also from the tens and hundreds columns. By the end of *Addition,* students can solve problems of this type:

```
    1818
    1943
    2775
 +   559
 ——————
```

Subtraction

The *Subtraction* module begins with problems that do not require regrouping (borrowing). Students learn basic conventions, such as starting with the ones column and subtracting the bottom number from the top number. Next, students are introduced to four preskills for borrowing. They learn which column to borrow from, how to rewrite a number after borrowing, when to borrow, and how to subtract after borrowing. Finally, students learn how to work four types of borrowing problems: borrowing from one column, borrowing from zero, borrowing from consecutive columns, and borrowing from as many as three consecutive columns. By the end of the *Subtraction* module, student can solve problems of these types:

```
    6824          4926          4000
 -  1904       -  3749       -   245
 ——————        ——————        ——————
```

Multiplication

The *Multiplication* module begins with noncarrying column problems and horizontal problems with counters. Then, students are introduced to carrying. They write the number being carried in a box at the top of the tens column. Next, students are introduced to multiplying by 2-digit numbers. Initially, students multiply only by the tens number (the ones number has already been done for them). Finally, students work the entire problem. By the end of *Multiplication,* students can solve problems like these:

```
    265          241          503
 ×   93       ×   50       ×   48
 ——————        ——————        ——————
```

Division

The division operation is first introduced for single-digit divisor problems. Students underline the part of the dividend that is at least as big as the divisor. Next, they work the underlined problem and find the remainder for that part. Then, they bring down the next digit and work the new problem in the same way. They continue in this manner until they have written a number above the last digit of the dividend. This signals that the problem is finished.

The single-digit divisor strategy is first shown with problems that have 1- and 2-digit answers. Early problems do not have answers with zeros. Later problems present 3-digit answers, answers with zero in the middle, and answers with zero as the final digit. Special exercises focus on these troublesome types of division problems.

For 2-digit divisors, the procedure is the same as that for single-digit divisors, except the students round off the divisor and the underlined part of the problem to the nearest tens number. For example, if the problem is $63\overline{)483}$, students write the rounded-off problem as $6\overline{)48}$. The rounding-off sometimes leads to trial answers that are either too large or too small. Students are taught to determine whether the remainder is too large, and if it is, to make the answer larger. If the remainder is too small (a negative number), students make the answer smaller. By the end of the module, students can solve problems of these types:

$44\overline{)5900}$ $24\overline{)2165}$

$34\overline{)3618}$ $75\overline{)3052}$

Problem-Solving Routines

The most important feature of the operations portions of these modules is that the problem-solving routines are introduced only after you have taught all preskills necessary for errorless student performance. For the students, the routines are simply procedural chains of familiar discriminations and responses, and success is ensured.

The care with which each necessary preskill is introduced is well demonstrated by the operations activities in the *Subtraction* module. Before the students learn the routine for subtracting with borrowing in one column, they master these preskills:

- **Rewriting numbers by borrowing.** Given a number with one digit slashed, the students learn to borrow from the slashed digit. The students write the borrowed amount in front of the digit immediately to the right of the slashed digit.

  Given   3572

  Students write   3⁄^{2}572

- **Subtracting multidigit numbers without borrowing.** Given a multidigit subtraction problem, the students learn to subtract the bottom digit from the top digit in each column, starting with the ones column.

  Given   841
  $$-\ 410$$

  Students begin with the ones column and write   841
  $$-\ 410$$
  $$431$$

- **Minusing zero when zero is not written.** Given a subtraction problem in which the minuend has more digits than the subtrahend, the students learn that the absence of a digit in the subtrahend means they must subtract zero.

  Given   348
  $$-\ \ \ \ 7$$

  Students write   348
  $$-\ \ \ \ 7$$
  $$341$$

- **Determining when and where to borrow.** Given a partial subtraction problem, the students learn that "if you're minusing more than you start with, you have to borrow." The students use a slash to indicate the position of the digit they would borrow from.

Given

$$\begin{array}{r} \square\,2\,\square \\ -\,\square\,7\,\square \\ \hline \end{array} \qquad \begin{array}{r} \square\square\,5\,\square \\ -\ \ \square\,3\,\square \\ \hline \end{array}$$

Students write

$$\begin{array}{r} \boxed{\diagup}\,2\,\square \\ -\,\square\,7\,\square \\ \hline \end{array} \qquad \begin{array}{r} \square\square\,5\,\square \\ -\ \ \square\,3\,\square \\ \hline \end{array}$$

- **Subtracting when borrowing has been done.** Given a problem in which borrowing has been done for the students, the students learn to subtract accurately.

Given

$$\begin{array}{r} 2 \\ \boxed{3}\,{}^{1}4 \\ -\,1\,8 \\ \hline \end{array}$$

Students write

$$\begin{array}{r} 2 \\ \boxed{3}\,{}^{1}4 \\ -\,1\,8 \\ \hline 1\,6 \end{array}$$

- **Practice borrowing.** Given a problem requiring borrowing, students learn to rewrite the digits in the minuend.

Given

$$\begin{array}{r} 5\,2 \\ -\,3\,6 \\ \hline \end{array}$$

Students write

$$\begin{array}{r} 4 \\ \cancel{5}\,{}^{1}2 \\ -\,3\,6 \\ \hline \end{array}$$

Only after the students have mastered all six preskills are they introduced to the borrowing routine.

1. The students read the problem in the ones column.

2. The students determine whether they have to borrow.

3. If borrowing is necessary, they
   A. Determine which number to borrow from.
   B. Slash that number, and write the number that is left.
   C. Write a 1 in front of the number to the right of the number borrowed from.
   D. Reread the problem in the ones column, and subtract.

The same care is taken later in the *Subtraction* module when teaching the preskills required for borrowing from consecutive columns and borrowing from zero. The same care is also taken in *Addition, Multiplication,* and *Division* modules. In every case, all necessary preskills are taught before problem-solving routines are introduced.

Story Problems Track

One of the major strengths of the *Corrective Mathematics* program is that *Corrective Mathematics* teaches a precise strategy for determining which mathematics operation is required by a given story problem—a feature not typically shared by other mathematics programs.

Story problems are introduced in the *Addition* module through three major exercises: working with pictures, working with sentences in columns, and working with sentences in paragraphs.

Addition story problems include distracters, numbers that appear but are not used in computing the answer. Two types of distracters are presented: distracters that involve the wrong class of object and those that involve the wrong verb. Here is an example of a story problem with a distracter that is from the "wrong class of objects" (rosebushes).

There are 528 apple trees. There are 4108 cherry trees. There are 180 rosebushes. There are 600 oak trees. How many trees are there?

Here is an example of a story problem with two verbs that distract, that are irrelevant to the operation *(built, rode)*.

> 261 teachers went swimming. 493 students built forts. 97 parents went swimming. 135 students rode bikes. 2580 children went swimming. How many people went swimming?

Although students learn in the *Subtraction* module that certain verbs generally indicate whether to add *(find, get, buy)* or subtract *(lose, give away, break)*, they quickly learn that they cannot rely solely on the verb to determine the appropriate operation. For example, the following problem calls for addition, even though *give away* would seemingly call for subtraction.

> Bill gives away 4 toys. John gives away 2 toys. How many toys did the boys give away?

Because using the verb to determine whether addition or subtraction is called for is not a viable strategy for many story problems, the *Subtraction* module quickly teaches this discrimination strategy: If the problem gives the big number, it's a subtraction problem; if the problem does not give the big number, it's an addition problem. (The "big number" is the minuend in a subtraction problem and the sum in an addition problem.) The strategy is illustrated by the following problems.

> Mr. Yamada had 36 books. Last week he bought more books at the used bookstore. Now he has 58 books. How many books did he buy last week?

In this problem, the big number, 58, is given. Therefore, the problem is a subtraction problem and translates into

$$\begin{array}{r} 58 \\ -\ 36 \\ \hline \end{array}$$

In the second problem, the big number (how many windows in all) is not given.

> An office building has 2365 clean windows. The window washers have to wash 90 dirty windows. How many windows in all does the building have?

Therefore, the problem is an addition problem and translates into

$$\begin{array}{r} 2365 \\ +\ \ \ \ 90 \\ \hline \end{array}$$

In the *Multiplication* module, the students are taught that "if you use the same number again and again, you multiply."

> There are 9 alarm clocks, 9 wall clocks, and 9 grandfather clocks in the shop. How many clocks are there in all?

In this problem, the same number is used again and again. The problem is a multiplication problem and translates into

$$9 \times 3 =$$

If the same number is not used again and again, the problem is not a multiplication problem. It must be an addition or a subtraction problem.

> There are 5 green flowers, 4 red flowers, and 2 blue flowers in bloom. How many flowers are there in all?

Because the big number is not given, the problem is an addition problem and translates into

$$\begin{array}{r} 5 \\ 4 \\ +\ 2 \\ \hline \end{array}$$

Students also learn that the words *each* and *every* signal that the same number is being used again and again. This problem, therefore, is a multiplication problem.

There are 9 books on each shelf. There are 3 shelves. How many books are there in all?

In the *Division* module, the discrimination strategy is expanded. The students learn to apply two tests to story problems.

1. If the same number is used again and again, the problem is either a multiplication problem or a division problem. If the same number is not used again and again, it's an addition or a subtraction problem.

2. In problems involving multiplication or division, the problem requires division if the big number is given and multiplication if the big number is not given. In problems involving addition or subtraction, the problem requires subtraction if the big number is given and addition if the big number is not given.

In the problem below, the same number is used again and again, so the problem is either multiplication or division.

> Every day Mattie read 3 books. Mattie read 18 books in all. How many days did Mattie read books?

The big number is given, so the problem is a division problem that translates to

$$3\overline{)18}$$

The strategy ensures that the students will attend closely to all the words in a story problem, even in the *Addition* module where no discrimination between operations is possible.

An additional strength of the Story Problems track of the modules is that the students are taught to apply their discrimination strategies to a wide variety of problem types, such as in the *Subtraction* module.

- **Simple Action.** A "subtraction verb," *broken,* calls for subtraction.

  Ann found 206 pencils. 78 of the pencils were broken. How many of the pencils were not broken?

- **Complex Action.** An "addition verb," *built,* calls for subtraction.

  There were 143 cabins at the lake. This year more cabins were built. Now there are 160 cabins. How many more cabins were built at the lake?

- **Classification.** Numbers for the smaller classes are added.

  The shop had 86 apples and 90 oranges. How many pieces of fruit did the shop have?

- **Comparison.** Younger age is subtracted from older age.

  Ms. Savas is 42 years old. Ms. Hark is 70 years old. How many years older is Ms. Hark?

Furthermore, the specific preskills for each problem type are carefully taught. For instance, before being presented with addition and subtraction classification problems, the students are taught the class name for the big number. In a problem involving hammers, tools, and saws, students are taught that *tool* is the name for the big number because hammers are tools and saws are tools.

Place-Value Track

In the *Addition, Subtraction,* and *Multiplication* modules, students learn about place value. They are taught to read numbers as long as five digits and to write these numbers, putting commas in appropriate places. They learn to deal with numbers that include one or more zeros. They receive practice in identifying the digits in a number as belonging to the ones, tens, hundreds, or thousands columns. The students then learn to write dictated numbers in columns with the digits properly aligned.

```
426
 32
 12
634
```

Scope and Sequence Chart
Addition

	1	5	10	15	20	25	30	35	40	45	50	55	60	65

Facts

Skill	Range
Determine the sum of any two 1-digit numbers.	1 → 65
Write two facts as any two given 1-digit numbers.	1 → 65
Say a series of consecutively ordered facts. For example, 7 + 1 = 8, 7 + 2 = 9, 7 + 3 = 10.	10 → 65
Determine the sum of a 2-digit number plus a 1-digit number. The digit in the tens column of the sum is the same as the digit in the tens column of the 2-digit addend. For example, 14 + 5 = 19.	20 → 65 (Teach ~35–65)
Determine the sum of a 2-digit number plus a 1-digit number. The digit in the tens column of the sum is one ten greater than the digit in the tens column of the 2-digit addend. For example, 14 + 8 = 22.	30 → 65

Place Value

Skill	Range
Say the number for a 3-digit numeral.	1 → 65
Write the numeral for any 2- or 3-digit number.	15 → 65
Say the number for a 4-digit numeral.	30 → 65
Say the number of tens in a 2-digit numeral.	30 → 65
Write the numeral for any 4-digit number.	45 → 65

Operations

Skill	Range
Determine the sum of two 2- or 3-digit numbers. No regrouping. Vertical format.	10 → 65
Determine the sum of two 2- or 3-digit numbers. No regrouping. Horizontal format.	10 → 65
Determine the sum of three or four single-digit numbers. With and without regrouping.	10 → 65
Determine the sum of three or four 2-digit numbers. No regrouping.	20 → 65
Determine the sum of three or four 1- or 2-digit numbers. The sum of the ones column is greater than 9.	20 → 65
Determine the sum of three or four 1-, 2-, or 3-digit numbers. The sum of the ones column as well as the sum of the tens column is greater than 9. Regrouping required.	30 → 65
Determine the sum of three or four 1-, 2-, 3-, or 4-digit numbers. The sums of the ones, tens, and/or hundreds columns are between 10 and 20. Regrouping required.	40 → 65
Determine the sum of three or four 2-, 3-, or 4-digit numbers. The sums of the ones, tens, and/or hundreds columns are between 10 and 35. Regrouping required.	50 → 65

Story Problems

Skill	Range
Determine the sum in a story problem with extraneous information. (Picture problems.)	20 → 65
Determine the sum in a story problem with extraneous information. (Sentences in columns.)	25 → 65
Determine the sum in a story problem with extraneous information. (Paragraph form.)	40 → 65

Key: Teach ▬▬▬▬▬   Review ▬▬▬▬▬

Scope and Sequence Chart

Subtraction

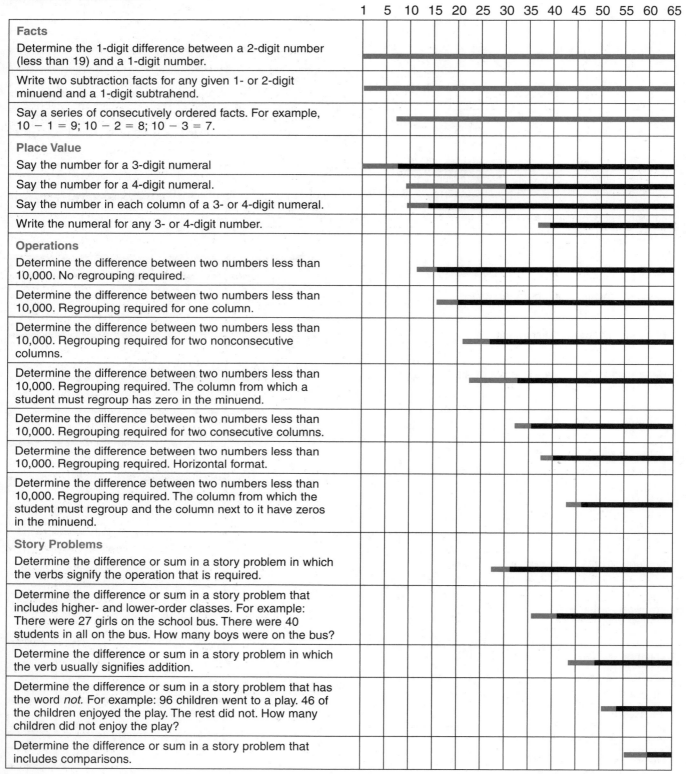

	1	5	10	15	20	25	30	35	40	45	50	55	60	65
Facts														
Determine the 1-digit difference between a 2-digit number (less than 19) and a 1-digit number.														
Write two subtraction facts for any given 1- or 2-digit minuend and a 1-digit subtrahend.														
Say a series of consecutively ordered facts. For example, $10 - 1 = 9$; $10 - 2 = 8$; $10 - 3 = 7$.														
Place Value														
Say the number for a 3-digit numeral														
Say the number for a 4-digit numeral.														
Say the number in each column of a 3- or 4-digit numeral.														
Write the numeral for any 3- or 4-digit number.														
Operations														
Determine the difference between two numbers less than 10,000. No regrouping required.														
Determine the difference between two numbers less than 10,000. Regrouping required for one column.														
Determine the difference between two numbers less than 10,000. Regrouping required for two nonconsecutive columns.														
Determine the difference between two numbers less than 10,000. Regrouping required. The column from which a student must regroup has zero in the minuend.														
Determine the difference between two numbers less than 10,000. Regrouping required for two consecutive columns.														
Determine the difference between two numbers less than 10,000. Regrouping required. Horizontal format.														
Determine the difference between two numbers less than 10,000. Regrouping required. The column from which the student must regroup and the column next to it have zeros in the minuend.														
Story Problems														
Determine the difference or sum in a story problem in which the verbs signify the operation that is required.														
Determine the difference or sum in a story problem that includes higher- and lower-order classes. For example: There were 27 girls on the school bus. There were 40 students in all on the bus. How many boys were on the bus?														
Determine the difference or sum in a story problem in which the verb usually signifies addition.														
Determine the difference or sum in a story problem that has the word *not.* For example: 96 children went to a play. 46 of the children enjoyed the play. The rest did not. How many children did not enjoy the play?														
Determine the difference or sum in a story problem that includes comparisons.														

Key: Teach ▬▬▬ Review ▬▬▬

Scope and Sequence Chart
Multiplication

Column scale: 1 5 10 15 20 25 30 35 40 45 50 55 60 65

Skill	Teach (approx. range)	Review (approx. range)
Facts		
Determine the product of two 1-digit numbers.	1–65	—
Write two multiplication facts for any two 1-digit numbers.	1–65	—
Say a series of consecutively ordered facts. For example, $5 \times 5 = 25$; $5 \times 6 = 30$.	5–65	—
Determine the sum of a 2-digit number and a 1-digit number.	10–37	37–65
Determine the product of two 1-digit numbers, one of which is zero.	32–35	35–65
Place Value		
Say the number for a 3-digit numeral.	1–12	—
Say the number in each column of a 2-digit number.	13–16	16–65
Say the number for a 4-digit numeral.	13–17	17–65
Say the number for a 5-digit numeral.	45–48	48–65
Operations		
Determine the product of a 2- or 3-digit number and a 1-digit number. No regrouping required.	20–23	23–65
Determine the product of a 2-digit number and a 1-digit number. Regrouping required.	18–21	21–65
Determine the product of a 3-digit number and a 1-digit number. Regrouping required for two columns.	25–28	28–65
Determine the product of two 2-digit numbers.	30–35	35–50
Determine the product of a 2-digit number and a 3-digit number.	45–48	48–65
Determine the product of a 2-digit number and a 1-digit number. The multiplier has a zero in the ones column.	50–53	53–65
Story Problems		
Determine the product or sum in a story problem with two 1-digit numbers.	30–33	33–65
Determine the product or sum in a story problem with a 2- or 3-digit number and a 1-digit number.	38–40	40–65
Determine the product, sum, or difference in a story problem with a 2- or 3-digit number and a 1-digit number.	45–47	47–65
Determine the product, sum, or difference in a story problem with a 2-digit number and a 2- or 3-digit number.	53–55	55–65

Key: Teach ▬▬▬▬   Review ▬▬▬▬

Scope and Sequence Chart
Division

Scale (lessons): 1 5 10 15 20 25 30 35 40 45 50 55 60 65

Facts

- Write two division facts for any given 1- or 2-digit dividend and a 1-digit divisor.
- Determine the 1-digit quotient of a 1- or 2-digit dividend and a 1-digit divisor.
- Say a series of consecutively ordered facts. For example, $5\overline{)5}^{\,1}$, $5\overline{)10}^{\,2}$, $5\overline{)15}^{\,3}$.

Place Value

- Determine the approximation of a 2-digit number to the nearest ten.
- Determine the approximation of a 3-digit number to the nearest hundred.

Operations

- Determine the 1-digit quotient and remainder, if any, resulting from the division of a 1- or 2-digit number by a 1-digit number.
- Determine the 2-digit quotient and remainder, if any, resulting from the division of a 2- or 3-digit number by a 1-digit number.
- Determine the 3-digit quotient and remainder, if any, resulting from the division of a 3- or 4-digit number by a 1-digit number.
- Determine the 2- or 3-digit quotient and remainder, if any, resulting from the division of a 3- or 4-digit number by a 1-digit number. Quotient has a zero in the tens and/or hundreds column.
- Determine the 4-digit quotient and remainder, if any, resulting from the division of a 4-digit number by a 1-digit number.
- Determine the 1- or 2-digit quotient and remainder, if any, resulting from the division of a 2- or 3-digit number by a 2-digit number.
- Determine the 3-digit quotient and remainder, if any, resulting from the division of a 4-digit number by a 2-digit number.

Story Problems

- Determine the quotient or product of 2 numbers in a story problem.
- Determine the sum or difference of 2 numbers in a story problem.
- Determine the quotient, product, sum, or difference of 2 numbers in a story problem.

Key: Teach ▬▬▬▬▬   Review ▬▬▬▬▬

◆ Basic Fractions

Overview of Skill Development

Concept of Fractions

Basic Fractions teaches what the numbers in a fraction tell. The bottom number tells how many parts in each whole, and the top number tells how many parts are used.

In the fraction $\frac{3}{4}$, there are 4 parts in each whole, and 3 parts are used.

Students are shown how to apply these rules in exercises that require them to fill in the numbers to represent a picture and in exercises that require them to write a diagram that represents a numerical fraction. Exercises include diagrams showing fractions that

- ◆ equal less than 1 whole

$\frac{3}{4}$ $\frac{2}{3}$

- ◆ equal 1 whole

$\frac{2}{2}$ $\frac{5}{5}$

- ◆ equal more than 1 whole

$\frac{5}{3}$

Operations on Fractions

The modules present visual demonstrations of what happens when fractions are added. The initial exercises presenting adding fractions with like denominators show diagrams like this:

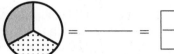

The students write 3 on the bottom because there are 3 parts in each whole. Then they write the 4 + 1 on the top. The 4 represents the 4 shaded parts, and the 1 represents the dotted part. The students then add the 4 + 1 and write 5. The solved problem looks like this:

 $= \dfrac{4+1}{3} = \boxed{\dfrac{5}{3}}$

There are no diagrams in the next exercise. The students are shown problems such as this:

$$\frac{3}{4} + \frac{2}{4} = \underline{\hspace{1.5em}} = \boxed{\frac{}{}}$$

The student writes

$$\frac{3}{4} + \frac{2}{4} = \frac{3+2}{4} = \boxed{\frac{5}{4}}$$

Worksheet exercises include several addition and subtraction problems with like denominators and some problems with unlike denominators. In *Basic Fractions*, students simply cross out the problems with unlike denominators because they cannot add or subtract when the fractions do not have the same number of parts in each whole. Addition and subtraction of fractions with unlike denominators are taught in *Fractions, Decimals, and Percents*.

After students have had a great deal of practice adding and subtracting fractions, problems requiring multiplication are introduced. Extensive practice is provided to enable students to master the difference between the procedure to solve multiplication problems (top times top and bottom times bottom) and the procedures used to solve addition and subtraction problems. Delaying the introduction of multiplying fractions until students have practiced adding and subtracting fractions decreases the chances of students becoming confused.

$$\frac{4}{5} \times \frac{3}{4} = \boxed{\phantom{\frac{0}{0}}}$$

$$\frac{4}{5} \times \frac{3}{4} = \boxed{\frac{12}{}}$$

$$\frac{4}{5} \times \frac{3}{4} = \boxed{\frac{12}{20}}$$

Then *Basic Fractions* teaches students how to convert a whole number to a fraction by writing a denominator of 1. You make 9 into a fraction by writing 9 over 1:

$$\frac{9}{1}$$

This critical component skill is practiced before problems that require multiplying a whole number and a fraction are presented. When this type of problem is presented, students are taught to convert the whole number to a fraction and then to multiply top times top and bottom times bottom. This example is from Lesson 27.

EXERCISE 2

Multiplication

a. (Write on the board:)

$$3 \times \frac{5}{7} = \underline{} \qquad \frac{2}{3} \times 8 = \underline{}$$

b. (Point to the 3 in $3 \times \frac{5}{7}$)

- Let's change the number into a fraction so that we can multiply. Tell me how to write this number as a fraction. **(Signal.)** *3 over 1.*
- (Change 3 to $\frac{3}{1}$.)
- Now we can multiply. What's the answer for the top? **(Signal.)** *15.*
- (Write to show:)

$$\frac{3}{1} \times \frac{5}{7} = \frac{15}{}$$

- What's the answer for the bottom? **(Signal.)** *7.*
- (Write to show:)

$$\frac{3}{1} \times \frac{5}{7} = \frac{15}{7}$$

- What's the answer to the problem? **(Signal.)** *15 sevenths.*

Parts and Wholes

Basic Fractions teaches students the difference between parts of a whole and an entire whole. In early lessons, diagrams show fractions representing several wholes.

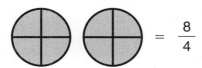 $= \dfrac{8}{4}$

Later, students learn to tell how many wholes a fraction equals by determining how many times bigger the top number is than the bottom number of a fraction. If the top number is 2 times bigger, the fraction equals 2 wholes. If the top number is 6 times bigger, the fraction equals 6 wholes. The following is part of an exercise from Lesson 42.

EXERCISE 3

Fractions to Wholes

a. (Write on the board:)

★

$$\dfrac{12}{4} \qquad \dfrac{15}{3} \qquad \dfrac{20}{2}$$

$$\dfrac{30}{5} \qquad \dfrac{20}{4}$$

b. These fractions are the same as numbers. We're going to figure out the amount that each fraction equals.
• Here's a rule about fractions: A fraction equals 2 wholes when the top is 2 times bigger than the bottom.
• A fraction equals 5 wholes when the top is 5 times bigger than the bottom.
• A fraction equals 6 wholes when the top is 6 times bigger than the bottom.
c. When does a fraction equal 3 wholes? (Signal.) *When the top is 3 times bigger than the bottom.*
• When does a fraction equal 9 wholes? (Signal.) *When the top is 9 times bigger than the bottom.*
• When does a fraction equal 7 wholes? (Signal.) *When the top is 7 times bigger than the bottom.*

d. (Point to $\dfrac{12}{4}$.)
• Let's figure out the number that this fraction equals. What's the bottom number? (Signal.) *4.*
• Tell me how many times bigger than 4 is the top. Get ready. (Signal.) *3.*

▶ **To Correct**

• (If the student has been taught to multiply by "count-bys," say:) Figure out how many times you would count by 4 to reach 12. (Pause.) What's the answer? (Signal.) *3.* ◀

▶ **To Correct**

• (If the student knows any other forms of multiplication, say:) Tell me 4 times how many equals 12. (Pause.) What's the answer? (Signal.) *3.* ◀
e. The top is 3 times bigger than the bottom. So how many wholes does the fraction equal? (Signal.) *3.*

• Yes, it equals 3 wholes.
• (Write to show:)

$$\dfrac{12}{4} = \boxed{3}$$

Mixed Numbers

Converting mixed numbers to fractions is introduced after students have learned and practiced finding the number of wholes in a fraction. To convert a mixed number to a fraction, the students learn first to write the fractional equivalent of the whole number and then to add the number of parts in the remaining whole. This example is from Lesson 45.

EXERCISE 4

Expanding Fractions

a. (Write on the board:)

$$2\frac{1}{3} =$$

b. We're going to change this mixed number into a fraction.

- (Point to the $\frac{}{3}$.)
- The bottom number of the fraction tells us that we will have 3 parts in each whole. So I write a 3.
- (Write to show:)

$$2\frac{1}{3} = \frac{}{3}$$

- (Touch the 2.)
- How many wholes do we have? (Signal.) *2.*
- A fraction equals 2 wholes when the top is 2 times bigger than the bottom. What's the bottom of the fraction we're writing? (Signal.) *3.*
- The top must be 2 times bigger than 3. Tell me that number for the top. Get ready. (Signal.) *6.*
- (Write to show:)

$$2\frac{1}{3} = \frac{6}{3}$$

- We used the 2 wholes.
- (Touch the $\frac{1}{}$.)
- How many parts are left? (Signal.) *1.*

- (Write to show:)

$$2\frac{1}{3} = \frac{6+1}{3}$$

- We have 6 plus one parts. How many parts do we have altogether? (Signal.) *7.*
- (Write to show:)

$$2\frac{1}{3} = \frac{6+1}{3} = \frac{7}{}$$

- How many parts are in each whole? (Signal.) *3.*
- (Write to show:)

$$2\frac{1}{3} = \frac{6+1}{3} = \frac{7}{3}$$

- What fraction does 2 and one third equal? (Signal.) *7 thirds.*

Equivalent Fractions

Students learn that equivalent fractions are created by multiplying a fraction by another fraction that equals 1. Two component skills exercises prepare students for equivalent fraction exercises.

The first component skill teaches students to identify fractions that equal 1 whole: A fraction equals 1 whole when you use the same number of parts that are in each whole.

$$\frac{4}{4} = \frac{7}{7} = \frac{9}{9} = 1$$

The second component skill teaches the concept that when you multiply by 1, you start and end with equal amounts.

$$\frac{3}{5} \times 1 = \frac{3}{5}$$

The initial exercises in which students are asked to find a missing number in an equivalent fraction are written in this form:

$$\frac{4}{5} \times \left(\ \right) = \frac{\ }{15}$$

The students will write a fraction equal to 1 in the parentheses. The equal sign indicates that we must end with an amount that equals the amount we start with. We must multiply $\frac{4}{5}$ by a fraction that equals 1. The students first figure out what number the denominator of the first fraction must be multiplied by to end up with the denominator of the second fraction. Five times what number equals 15? The answer is 3. The denominator of the fraction we're multiplying $\frac{4}{5}$ by is 3. Because we must multiply by a fraction that equals 1, the top number must also be 3. A fraction equals 1 when the top and the bottom numbers are the same. The students write $\frac{3}{3}$ in parentheses and then multiply the numerator of the initial fraction and the numerator of the fraction that equals 1 whole. The answer is 12.

$$\frac{4}{5} \times \left(\ \right) = \frac{12}{15}$$

Scope and Sequence Chart
Basic Fractions

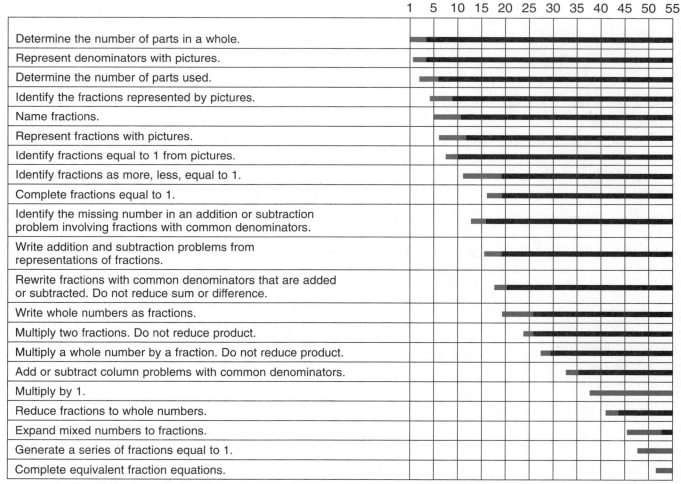

	1	5	10	15	20	25	30	35	40	45	50	55
Determine the number of parts in a whole.	■■■■■■■■■■■■■■■■■■■■■■■■■■■■■■											
Represent denominators with pictures.	■■■■■■■■■■■■■■■■■■■■■■■■■■■■■■											
Determine the number of parts used.	■■■■■■■■■■■■■■■■■■■■■■■■■■■■											
Identify the fractions represented by pictures.	■■■■■■■■■■■■■■■■■■■■■■■■■■											
Name fractions.	■■■■■■■■■■■■■■■■■■■■■■■■											
Represent fractions with pictures.	■■■■■■■■■■■■■■■■■■■■■■											
Identify fractions equal to 1 from pictures.	■■■■■■■■■■■■■■■■■■■■■■											
Identify fractions as more, less, equal to 1.	■■■■■■■■■■■■■■■■■											
Complete fractions equal to 1.	■■■■■■■■■■■■■■■											
Identify the missing number in an addition or subtraction problem involving fractions with common denominators.	■■■■■■■■■■■■■											
Write addition and subtraction problems from representations of fractions.	■■■■■■■■■■■											
Rewrite fractions with common denominators that are added or subtracted. Do not reduce sum or difference.	■■■■■■■■■											
Write whole numbers as fractions.	■■■■■■■											
Multiply two fractions. Do not reduce product.	■■■■■											
Multiply a whole number by a fraction. Do not reduce product.	■■■											
Add or subtract column problems with common denominators.	■■■											
Multiply by 1.	■■											
Reduce fractions to whole numbers.	■■											
Expand mixed numbers to fractions.	■											
Generate a series of fractions equal to 1.	■											
Complete equivalent fraction equations.	■											

Key: Teach ■■■■■■■■■■■■■■■■■■■■   Review ■■■■■■■■■■■■■■■■■■■■

◆ Fractions, Decimals, and Percents

Overview of Skill Development

Fractions, Decimals, and Percents is designed to teach advanced fraction skills and decimal and percent skills. *Fractions, Decimals, and Percents* builds on *Basic Fractions.*

Adding and Subtracting Fractions with Unlike Denominators

Students make the bottom numbers the same by figuring out the fraction equal to 1 by which they must multiply each original fraction.

$$\frac{3}{4} \quad \frac{3}{3} = \frac{9}{4 \times 3}$$

$$+ \frac{5}{3} \quad \frac{4}{4} = \frac{}{4 \times 3}$$

Reducing Fractions

Students learn to reduce a fraction by pulling out the largest possible fraction that equals 1.

$$\frac{12}{20} = \left(\frac{4}{4}\right) \times \frac{3}{5}$$

They learn to reduce an improper fraction by rewriting the fraction so that part of the numerator is a multiple of the denominator. They then write the multiple as a whole number.

$$\frac{32}{12} = \frac{24 + 8}{12} = 2\frac{8}{12}$$

Later, students put these reducing and rewriting skills together to change improper fractions to mixed fractions and reduce them.

$$\frac{24}{9} = 2\frac{6}{9}$$

$$\frac{6}{9} = \left(\frac{3}{3}\right) \times \frac{2}{3}$$

Dividing Fractions

Students learn to rewrite the problem as one fraction on top of the other fraction.

$$\frac{2}{3} \div \frac{4}{5} = \frac{\frac{2}{3}}{\frac{4}{5}}$$

Their goal is to get rid of the bottom fraction. The bottom fraction is changed into 1 by multiplying it by its inverse fraction.

$$\frac{\frac{2}{3}}{\frac{4}{5}} \quad \frac{5}{4}$$

Then the top is multiplied by the same fraction so that the original fraction is multiplied by 1.

$$\frac{\frac{2}{3}}{\frac{4}{5}} \left(\frac{\frac{5}{4}}{\frac{5}{4}}\right) = \frac{10}{12}$$

In Lesson 26, students learn the "invert and multiply" method.

$$\frac{2}{3} \div \frac{4}{5} = \frac{2}{3} \times \frac{5}{4} = \frac{10}{2}$$

Fraction Equivalencies

Because equivalent fractions are created by multiplying by fraction versions of 1, students can solve problems such as this.

$$\frac{2}{3} = \frac{10}{\square}$$

$$\xrightarrow{5}$$

$$\frac{2}{3} = \frac{10}{\boxed{15}}$$

$$\xrightarrow{5}$$

Decimal Notation

Students learn how to write fractions with denominators of 10, 100, and 1000 as decimals and how to write decimals as fractions.

Decimal Expansion

Students learn that adding zeros after the decimal point does not change the value of the decimal.

Operations

To add or subtract decimals, students make the same number of decimal places in each number and then line up the decimal points.

Students learn to multiply decimal numbers by 10, 100, and 1000 and learn the conventions of multiplying any two decimal numbers.

First students learn to divide a decimal number by a whole number. Then students learn to divide any number by a decimal or a mixed decimal.

Convert Fractions to Decimals to Percents

Students learn to change any fraction to a decimal and to handle any type of decimal-percent conversion.

Scope and Sequence Chart
Fractions, Decimals, and Percents

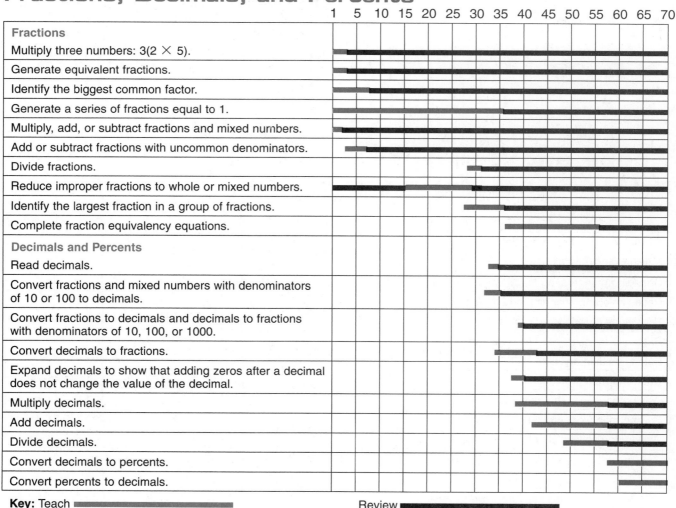

	1	5	10	15	20	25	30	35	40	45	50	55	60	65	70
Fractions															
Multiply three numbers: 3(2 × 5).															
Generate equivalent fractions.															
Identify the biggest common factor.															
Generate a series of fractions equal to 1.															
Multiply, add, or subtract fractions and mixed numbers.															
Add or subtract fractions with uncommon denominators.															
Divide fractions.															
Reduce improper fractions to whole or mixed numbers.															
Identify the largest fraction in a group of fractions.															
Complete fraction equivalency equations.															
Decimals and Percents															
Read decimals.															
Convert fractions and mixed numbers with denominators of 10 or 100 to decimals.															
Convert fractions to decimals and decimals to fractions with denominators of 10, 100, or 1000.															
Convert decimals to fractions.															
Expand decimals to show that adding zeros after a decimal does not change the value of the decimal.															
Multiply decimals.															
Add decimals.															
Divide decimals.															
Convert decimals to percents.															
Convert percents to decimals.															

Key: Teach ▬▬▬▬▬   Review ▬▬▬▬▬

◆ Ratios and Equations

Overview of Skill Development

Ratios and Equations is a 60-lesson program designed to teach basic ratio analysis and apply it to story problems. By understanding the procedure for changing any number into any other number by multiplying and how each number in a ratio (a pair of fractions) is related to each other number, the students can solve the following types of problems:

- $\frac{2}{3} A = 9$

- $2F = \frac{3}{4}$

- $\frac{1}{5} F = \square$

- $\frac{4}{9} = \frac{\frac{2}{3}}{\square}$

- 4 cows eat 3 tons of hay. How much do 7 cows eat?
- What is the rate of a plane that travels 850 kilometers in 3.4 hours?
- If it takes 5 men working 4 hours to build 3 meters of sidewalk, how long will it take 6 men to build 5 meters of sidewalk?
- What percent of 5 is 7?
- 30% of what number is 8?

Ratios and Equations is designed to be taught every day. The lessons average approximately 25 minutes. The module may be taught simultaneously with other skills, such as those needed later in the program—reducing factions, changing mixed numbers to fractions, decimal and fractional division, addition, and subtraction.

The program may be used by any student who has mastered at least fraction multiplication but who cannot solve problems involving ratios, simple equations, or ratio story problems. It may be used as a remedial program or as an introductory program.

Scope and Sequence Chart
Ratios and Equations
Major Tracks

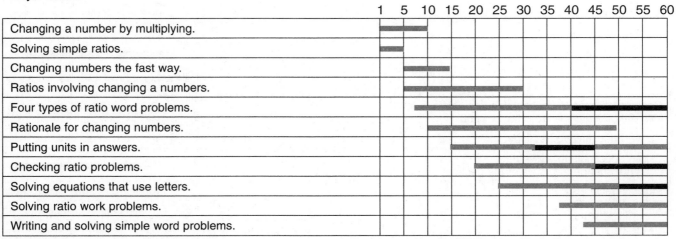

	1	5	10	15	20	25	30	35	40	45	50	55	60
Changing a number by multiplying.													
Solving simple ratios.													
Changing numbers the fast way.													
Ratios involving changing a numbers.													
Four types of ratio word problems.													
Rationale for changing numbers.													
Putting units in answers.													
Checking ratio problems.													
Solving equations that use letters.													
Solving ratio work problems.													
Writing and solving simple word problems.													

Key: Teach ▬▬▬▬▬▬▬▬▬▬   Review ▬▬▬▬▬▬

Placement Testing

Two Methods

There are two placement methods. You will use one of the methods to place students into the program.

The first and preferred method is to administer the *Corrective Mathematics* Comprehensive Placement Test, which is available on pages 31–35 and at sraonline.com.

The second placement method is to administer the preskill and placement tests that accompany each module. The preskill tests will determine whether a student should be placed in a particular module and, if so, at which lesson. Do not give these tests if you have already given the Comprehensive Placement Test.

- The Comprehensive Placement Test, found on page 31 of this guide and at sraonline.com, provides a short screening tool for placing students in SRA's *Corrective Mathematics* series. It will determine the correct entry point, both module and lesson, for each student.
  Most students enter *Corrective Mathematics* based on the results of the Comprehensive Placement Test.

- The module-specific tests and pretests are found in the corresponding Teacher's Presentation Book and at sraonline.com. The preskill test indicates whether students have the prerequisite skills needed to work in the module. The placement tests indicate which entry point is appropriate or whether students are too advanced to be placed in the module. Because placement tests indicate whether students have mastered the skills taught in the module, they can also be used as pre- and post-tests to assess growth.

The module-specific tests are used in place of the Comprehensive Placement Test if you are considering using one module to address a previously identified skill deficit. They can also be used to confirm results of the Comprehensive Placement Test if you question students' performance on the shorter screening instrument.

- The Comprehensive Placement Test will determine the module in which the students should begin the *Corrective Mathematics* series and the specific lesson on which the students should start. The test will also identify those students who are too advanced for any of the *Corrective Mathematics* modules as well as those students who are too low for any module in the series.

With one exception, all the tests are written tests that may be administered individually or to a group. The exception is the Addition Preskill Test. It is given to students who make many errors on the placement test that accompanies the *Addition* module or on the addition portion of the Comprehensive Placement Test. The Addition Preskill Test is an oral test and must be administered individually. It is designed to identify those students who are too low for any module in the *Corrective Mathematics* series.

There are two points to keep in mind when using either placement method. Students who do poorly on the placement test but have previously done well on the mathematics portion of any standardized achievement test should be reevaluated after a week or two of instruction. If these students are doing exceptionally well in the series, readminister the placement test. A skip to a later lesson or to a more advanced module might be indicated.

A second caution involves older students who test into the *Addition* module only because of difficulties with story problems. These students should be placed in the *Subtraction* module rather than in the *Addition* module.

Comprehensive Placement Test for *Corrective Mathematics*

The *Corrective Mathematics* Comprehensive Placement Test provides a gauge for placing students in SRA's *Corrective Mathematics* series. The Comprehensive Placement Test will determine the correct entry point (both module and lesson) for each student. If the Comprehensive Placement Test is used, it's not necessary to administer the preskill test or the placement tests that are included in the Workbook of each module.

For your convenience, the test is divided into two sections. **Section I** includes: Part A, Addition; Part B, Subtraction; Part C, Multiplication; and Part D, Division. **Section II** includes: Part E, Basic Fractions; Part F, Fractions, Decimals, and Percents; and Part G, Ratios and Equations.

Section I

During two sessions, administer the test either to the entire group or to individuals.

- During the first session, the students will work Parts A and B of the test (addition and subtraction). Allow 20 minutes for this session.
- Give Parts C and D only to those students who make no more than one error on Part A or B. Allow 20 minutes for the second session.

Administration and Scoring of Section I

Step 1
- Make copies of the Comprehensive Placement Test pages for Parts A–D. Distribute the copies.
- Tell the students not to start until you instruct them to start.
- Ask the students to fill in the information called for at the top of the test.

Step 2
- (Tell the students:)
  You're going to work Parts A and B of the test today. You'll have 20 minutes.

- Do all the problems you can. Work the problems right on the test sheet. If you have trouble with a problem, skip it and go on to the next problem.
- Read each problem carefully before you work it.
- Remember to do only Parts A and B. Start now.
- (After 20 minutes, tell the students to stop and hand in their tests.)

Step 3
Grade Parts A and B. There are 11 scorable items in Part A and 13 scorable items in Part B.

Look at the answer key that follows. Notice that there is more than one scorable item for some of the problems the students work.

- For all column problems, each column is scored separately. Each column on the answer key is labeled as an item. The answer for each item is in boldface. The first problem counts as one item because there is only one column. The sixth problem counts as four items (8, 9, 10, 11) because there are four columns.
- Each story problem counts as one item.

Answer Key
Part A *Addition*

(Problem 1)

(Problem 6)

Answer Key
Part B *Subtraction*

items ① ② ③ ④ ⑤

  4 8 3

          7 6
        − 1 8
          5 8

items ⑥ ⑦   ⑧ ⑨

  6 2   9 4
  − 5   − 2 8
  5 7   6 6

items ⑩ ⑪ ⑫ ⑬

  234 176 128 154

- Count the errors for Part A, and enter the total in the box following the heading "Errors" on the student's test packet.
- Count the errors for Part B, and enter the total in the box following the heading "Errors" on the student's test packet
- Do not administer Parts C and D of the Comprehensive Placement Test to the students who make more than one error on Part A or B. Place those students in either the *Addition* or the *Subtraction* module. See the Placement Directions for specific placement instructions.

Step 4

- Arrange another testing session, and present Parts C and D of the Comprehensive Placement Test. Follow the procedure outlined in Steps 1 and 2. Allow the students up to 20 minutes to complete the test.

Step 50

- Grade Parts C and D of the Comprehensive Placement Test. Notice that on these parts the entire answer to each problem counts as one item. Unit names are not required.

Answer Key
Part C *Multiplication*

15   8   27 or 27 hours
9 or 9 miles   12 or 12 chairs
387   90   10,935   2106   10,560

Part D *Division*

4   3   8 or 8 days
4 or 4 hours   4 or 4 times
34 R2   24   56 R6
60 R27   28 R58

Step 6

- Place students who make more than one error on Parts C or D in either the *Multiplication* or the *Division* module. (See Placement Directions.)
- If students make no more than one error on either Part C or D, have them take Parts E, F, and G of the Comprehensive Placement Test. See page 29 for directions.

Placement Directions for *Corrective Mathematics: Addition, Subtraction, Multiplication,* and *Division*

Part A—*Addition*

Total Errors	Lesson
8, 9, 10, or 11	Administer the *Addition* Preskill Test on page 28. Begin with Lesson 1 if Preskill Test is passed.
6 or 7	Present Transition Lesson 8 in the *Addition* Teacher's Presentation Book, and then begin instruction in the *Addition* module at Lesson 8.
2, 3, 4, or 5	Present Transition Lesson 23 in the *Addition* Teacher's Presentation Book, and then begin instruction in the *Addition* module at Lesson 23.
0 or 1	These students are too proficient for the *Addition* module. See the chart to determine whether they should be placed in the *Subtraction* module.

The Addition Preskill Test

The Addition Preskill Test is given to students who made 8 or more errors on Part A of the Placement Test. This test is individually administered and requires about five minutes. It tests students on their ability to count and to identify two-digit numbers. Students who make no more than one error on each section of the test should enter the module at Lesson 1. Students who exceed the error limit should not be placed in the module. *Distar®, Arithmetic I* or *Connecting Math Concepts* would be more appropriate for these students.

Following is the script that should be used for administering the Addition Preskill Test.

Part A

a. (Write the following numbers on the board or on a sheet of paper:)

17 32 18 56 90 12 39 81

b. (Point to 17.) Read the number. (Signal.) *17.*

c. (Repeat step b for the rest of the numbers.)

Part B

a. I'm going to count. When I stop counting I want you to keep counting until I tell you to stop.

b. 7, 8, 9. (Stop the students when they reach 15.)

c. 16, 17, 18. (Stop the students when they reach 22.)

d. 36, 37, 38. (Stop the students when they reach 41.)

e. 88, 89. (Stop the students when they reach 93.)

Part B—*Subtraction*

Total Errors	Lesson
11, 12, or 13	Begin with Lesson 1 in the *Subtraction* module.
5, 6, 7, 8, 9, or 10	Present Transition Lesson 8 in the *Subtraction* Teacher's Presentation Book, and then begin instruction in the *Subtraction* module at Lesson 8.
2, 3, or 4	Present Transition Lesson 25 in the *Subtraction* Teacher's Presentation Book, and then begin instruction in the *Subtraction* module at Lesson 25.
0 or 1	These students are too proficient for the *Subtraction* module. Test the students on Parts C and D of the Comprehensive Placement Test.

Part C—*Multiplication*

Total Errors	Lesson
9 or 10	Begin with Lesson 1 in the *Multiplication* module.
5, 6, 7, or 8	Present Transition Lesson 10 in the *Multiplication* Teacher's Presentation Book, and then begin instruction in the *Multiplication* module at Lesson 10.
2, 3, or 4	Present Transition Lesson 27 in the *Multiplication* Teacher's Presentation Book, and then begin instruction in the *Multiplication* module at Lesson 25.
0 or 1	These students are too proficient for *Multiplication*. See the following chart to determine whether they should be placed in *Division*.

Part D—*Division*

Total Errors	Lesson
9 or 10	Begin with Lesson 1 in the *Division* module module.
5, 6, 7, or 8	Present Transition Lesson 6 in the *Division* Teacher's Presentation Book, and then begin instruction in the *Division* module at Lesson 6.
2, 3, or 4	Present Transition Lesson 27 in the *Division* Teacher's Presentation Book, and then begin instruction in the *Division* module at Lesson 27.
0 or 1	These students are too proficient for the *Division* module. Test the students on Section II (Parts E, F, G) of the Comprehensive Placement Test.

Section II

During one session, administer the test either to the entire group or to individuals.

Administration and Scoring of Section II

Step 1
- Make copies of the Comprehensive Placement Test pages for Parts E–G. Distribute the copies.
- Tell the students not to start until you instruct them to start.
- Ask the students to fill in the information called for at the top of the test.

Step 2
- (Tell the students:)
  You're going to work Parts E, F, and G of the test today. You'll have 40 minutes to complete the test.
- You may work the problems on a separate sheet of paper, but be sure to write your answers on the test.
- Do all the problems you can. Work the problems right on the test sheet. If you have trouble with a problem, skip it and go on to the next problem.
- Read each problem carefully before you work it.

- Start now.
- (After 40 minutes, tell the students to stop and hand in their tests.)

Step 3
Grade Section II. Notice that in Part G the answers are not incorrect if the student did not include the word as part of the answer.

Answer Key
Part E *Basic Fractions*

1.   2. $\dfrac{6}{7}$ 3. $\dfrac{8}{8}$ or 1

4. $\dfrac{6}{4}$ or $\dfrac{3}{2}$ or $1\dfrac{2}{4}$ or $1\dfrac{1}{2}$ 5. $\dfrac{8}{7}$ or $1\dfrac{1}{7}$

6. $\dfrac{23}{4}$ 7. $\dfrac{22}{5}$ 8. $\dfrac{27}{10}$ or $2\dfrac{7}{10}$

Part F *Fractions, Decimals, and Percents*

1. $\dfrac{17}{6}$ or $2\dfrac{5}{6}$ 2. $\dfrac{2}{3}$ 3. $3\dfrac{3}{4}$

4. $\dfrac{6}{8}$ or $\dfrac{3}{4}$ 5. 20   6. 11.529

7. 87.5% or $87\dfrac{1}{2}$%

Part G *Ratios and Equations*

1. $\dfrac{21}{20}$ or $1\dfrac{1}{20}$ or 1.05 meters

2. $\dfrac{350}{12}$ or $29\dfrac{2}{12}$ or $29\dfrac{1}{6}$ meters

3. 6R = 18 or R = 3, 6R = 18

4. 60

5. $\dfrac{10}{3}$ or $3\dfrac{1}{3}$ or 3.33 meters

Placement Directions for *Corrective Mathematics:*
Basic Fractions; Fractions, Decimals, and Percents; and *Ratios and Equations*

Part E—*Basic Fractions*

Total Errors	Lesson
6, 7, or 8	Begin with Lesson 1 in *Basic Fractions*.
4 or 5	Begin with Lesson 19 in *Basic Fractions*.
2 or 3	Begin with Lesson 30 in *Basic Fractions*.
0 or 1	These students are too proficient for *Basic Fractions*. See the following chart to determine whether they should be placed in *Fractions, Decimals, and Percents*.

Part F—*Fractions, Decimals, and Percents*

Total Errors	Lesson
5, 6, or 7	Begin with Lesson 1 in *Fractions, Decimals, and Percents*.
2, 3, or 4	Begin with Lesson 30 in *Fractions, Decimals, and Percents*.
0 or 1	These students are too proficient for *Fractions, Decimals, and Percents*. See the following chart to determine whether they should be placed in *Ratios and Equations*.

Part G—*Ratios and Equations*

Total Errors	Lesson
3, 4, or 5	Begin with Lesson 1 in *Ratios and Equations*.
0, 1, or 2	These students are too proficient for *Ratios and Equations*.

Corrective Mathematics
Comprehensive Placement Test

Section I Parts A and B

Name _____ Class _____ Date _____

School _____ Tester _____

Part A

Errors [ ]

7	9	4	23	31	1393
+ 1	+ 1	+ 1	32	22	616
			50	52	9482
			+ 21	+ 41	+ 434

Part B

Errors [ ]

5	9	6	76	62	94
− 1	− 1	− 3	− 18	− 5	− 28

There are 189 red cars and 423 blue cars.
How many more blue cars are there than red cars?

The shop gave away 86 apples. The shop gave away 90 oranges.
How many pieces of fruit did the shop give away?

Ann found 206 pencils. 78 of the pencils were broken.
How many of the pencils were not broken?

146 girls go to our school. There are 300 children altogether in our school.
How many boys go to our school?

Stop.

Corrective Mathematics
Comprehensive Placement Test

Section I Part C

Name _____ Class _____ Date _____

School _____ Tester _____

Part C

$$\begin{array}{r} 5 \\ \times\,3 \\ \hline \end{array} \qquad \begin{array}{r} 2 \\ \times\,4 \\ \hline \end{array}$$

Jill worked 3 hours every day. She worked 9 days.
How many hours did she work altogether?

Ann ran 5 miles on Monday. Then she ran 4 miles on Tuesday.
How many miles did she run altogether?

There are 3 chairs in each row. There are 4 rows of chairs.
How many chairs are there altogether?

$$\begin{array}{r} 43 \\ \times\;\;9 \\ \hline \end{array} \qquad \begin{array}{r} 45 \\ \times\;\;2 \\ \hline \end{array} \qquad \begin{array}{r} 405 \\ \times\;\;27 \\ \hline \end{array} \qquad \begin{array}{r} 54 \\ \times\;39 \\ \hline \end{array} \qquad \begin{array}{r} 264 \\ \times\;\;40 \\ \hline \end{array}$$

Corrective Mathematics
Comprehensive Placement Test

Section I Part D

Name _____ Class _____ Date _____

School _____ Tester _____

Part D _____ Errors [ ]

3)12   9)27

5 buses left Midville each day. 40 buses left in all.
How many days did buses leave Midville?

Fred typed 2 pages each hour. He typed 8 pages.
How many hours did he type?

Every time Betty went jogging, she ran 5 blocks.
She ran 20 blocks. How many times did she go
jogging?

3)104   9)216   48)2694

54)3267   82)2354

Stop.

Corrective Mathematics Comprehensive Placement Test

Section II Parts E and F

Name _____ Class _____ Date _____

School _____ Tester _____

Part E

Errors [ ]

1. Draw the picture for the fraction.

   $\dfrac{5}{3}$ = ◯ ◯

2. $\dfrac{4}{7} + \dfrac{2}{7} =$

3. $\dfrac{10}{8} - \dfrac{2}{8} =$

4. $\dfrac{2}{4} \times 3 =$

5. $\dfrac{2}{7} \times 4 =$

6. $5\dfrac{3}{4} = \dfrac{}{4}$

7. $4\dfrac{2}{5} = \dfrac{}{5}$

8. $4\dfrac{1}{2} \times \dfrac{3}{5} =$

Part F

Errors [ ]

1. $2\dfrac{1}{2} + \dfrac{1}{3}$

2. Reduce this fraction

   $\dfrac{14}{21} =$

3. Write this fraction as a mixed number.

   $\dfrac{15}{4} =$

4. $\dfrac{3}{8} \div \dfrac{1}{2}$

5. $\dfrac{4}{\boxed{}} = \dfrac{3}{15}$

6. $3.52 + 6 + 2.009 =$

7. $\dfrac{7}{8} = \qquad \%$

Corrective Mathematics
Comprehensive Placement Test

Section II Part G

Name _____ Class _____ Date _____

School _____ Tester _____

Part G _____ Errors ☐

1. An oak tree is 5 meters high and makes a $\frac{3}{4}$ meter shadow. A maple tree is 7 meters high. How many meters is its shadow?

2. Pam runs 50 meters in 12 seconds, how far can she run in 7 seconds?

3. $3.5R = 10.5$
   Figure out what 6R equals.

4. 15% of what number is 9?

5. If 3 boxes contain $2\frac{1}{2}$ meters of wire, how long is the wire in 4 boxes?

Stop.

General Information

The Lesson

The Teacher Presentation Book contains daily lessons. The lessons are divided into exercises. Students earn points for some of these exercises. At the end of each lesson, the points are totaled.

The daily lesson is structured as follows:

Teacher-Directed Activities: Teacher-directed activities begin each lesson. Use the presentation materials, and follow the script there. Students respond to questions orally or by writing in their Workbooks. Some of these activities involve boardwork and are used to teach students new concepts and skills. The teacher-directed Workbook activities are used to practice and strengthen skills.

Mastery Test: Where applicable, administer, correct, and award points for the Mastery Tests.

Independent Work: In most lessons, students do a series of exercises on their own. These exercises provide the practice required to build proficiency.

Workcheck: Orally check Independent Work exercises. Award points.

Fact Game: In some *Addition, Subtraction, Multiplication,* and *Division* lessons there is a Fact Game that can be played anytime during the day. These games are used to ensure that students master basic addition, subtraction, multiplication and division facts.

Optional Facts-Practice Worksheets: These are blackline masters that are provided for additional facts practice in *Addition, Subtraction, Multiplication,* and *Division.* They may be used anytime during the day.

Cumulative Reviews and Review Lessons: The cumulative reviews are ongoing, cumulative practice. It is appropriate to use these sheets to reinforce skills presented in the *Addition, Subtraction, Multiplication,* and *Division* modules. One blackline master is provided for each two lessons, beginning with Lesson 2 and going through Lesson 64.

After the students have begun working on decimal skills in *Fractions, Decimals, and Percents,* there are periodic review lessons in their Workbook on adding, subtracting, multiplying, and dividing. If the students are not receiving continued practice on new fraction skills elsewhere, they should complete these review practices in Lessons 44, 49, 56, 63, 70, 71, and 72. Award 10 bonus points if students complete the review lessons.

Each lesson in the Teacher Presentation Book is laid out in the same way.

EXERCISE 1

Addition/Subtraction

a. Turn to Lesson 24 in your Workbook.
- Touch the first problem.
- Can you rewrite the fractions in that problem? (Signal.) *Yes.*
- How do you know? (Signal.) *The wholes are the same.*
- When you rewrite those fractions, what will you write on the bottom? (Signal.) *4.*
- What will you write on the top? (Signal.) *2 plus 7.*
- Rewrite the fractions. ✔
- Now you have to write the fraction in the box. How much does 2 plus 7 equal? (Signal.) *9.*
- Tell me the complete fraction you will write in the box. (Signal.) *9 fourths.*
- Write it. ✔

The heading tells what skills the students are working on.

What you **say** appears in blue.

(This type indicates what you do.)

This italic type indicates the students' response.

A check mark (✔) indicates that you quickly scan several students' work to see whether the students have followed directions.

Teaching Strategies

Introducing the Program

Before you begin the program, set aside a time for meeting with those students who will be in the program. This meeting is important for establishing a positive attitude toward what is going to happen and how it is going to happen. Students might have negative attitudes toward math, perhaps expressing the idea that something is wrong with them. During the initial meeting with the students, make these points clear:

1. The fact that these students are poor in mathematics is not an indication that they are not intelligent.

2. The only reason these students have trouble with math is that no one really taught them how to work the problems.

3. You are going to teach them to do the problems, but you do not have any magic way of doing it. You are responsible for working very hard to teach them, and they are responsible for working hard to learn.

Briefly describe the general rules about what the students will be doing during each lesson.

- They will work on math each day for about 30 minutes.
- When you ask questions, they will respond as a group unless you call on an individual.
- They will do the problems on their worksheets according to your instructions.
- They will correct any errors on their worksheets.

Classroom Arrangement

Seats should be arranged so that the front row of students is immediately in front of you as you stand at the board. You will write on the board as you teach the lesson.

Arrange the seating to ensure that low performers are seated near you and potential behavior-problem students are not sitting next to each other. A good plan is to arrange the room something like this:

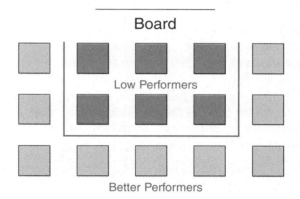

The lowest performers are closest to the front of the classroom. Better performers are arranged around the periphery because they need less observation and feedback. With this arrangement you can position yourself so that, by taking a few steps during the lesson, you can hear responses from soft-spoken students and monitor what students write.

Pacing

Each lesson contains many exercises. Therefore, each exercise must be taught quickly but not so quickly as to rush the students into making errors.

- Familiarize yourself with each lesson so it is not necessary to read each exercise word for word during the presentation.

- Present each exercise quickly, but never hurry students into making errors.
- Speak in a way that indicates to students that the information you are presenting is important.
- Never rush to finish a lesson in the allotted time at the expense of firming students on each activity.

With quickly paced lessons, you
- teach more in a given period of time.
- achieve better student attention and retention.
- encounter fewer management difficulties.

Signals

The goal of *Corrective Mathematics* is to teach every student. Therefore, you must receive clear feedback from each student. The fastest and most efficient way to get such information is to require all students to respond at the same time. A "signal" is a cue that all students should respond together. By using signals and group responses, you

- give students as many practice opportunities as possible during a lesson.
- receive accurate, diagnostic information about students' understanding.

If students are not required to respond in unison—some coming in early, some late, and some not at all, some students might simply copy the responses of others, and you will not get adequate feedback on student performance. When the program is presented in a positive manner and the teacher treats responding to signals as a very important convention, students of all ages adapt very well to group response on signal.

The simplest way to have students respond together is to use consistent timing—just like timing in a musical piece.

- Talk first.
- Pause one second.
- Then signal.

On some exercises, the students need time to think or time to count. You have to pause to give the students that time. Places you must pause are marked like this: (Pause.) Pause for 3 to 6 seconds whenever you see the pause sign, say "get ready," and then signal.

Hand-Drop Signal The hand-drop signal is used for exercises that you present orally with students looking at you.

1. Hold out your hand (as if you're stopping traffic) while you are saying the instructions or presenting the question.
2. Continue to hold your hand still for 1 second after you have completed the instructions or the question.
3. Then quickly drop your hand. Students should respond the instant your hand drops.

EXERCISE 3

Facts: Preskill for Minus-1 Facts

a. I'll say a number. You say the number that is 1 less. 7. What number is 1 less than 7? (Signal.) *6.*
b. 3. What number is 1 less than 3? (Signal.) *2.*
c. 10. What number is 1 less than 10? (Signal.) *9.*
d. 25. What number is 1 less than 25? (Signal.) *24.*
e. 7. What number is 1 less than 7? (Signal.) *6.*
f. 13. What number is 1 less than 13? (Signal.) *12.*
g. 37. What number is 1 less than 37? (Signal.) *36.*
h. (Repeat steps b–g until firm.)

Audible Signal This signal is used when students are attending to material on their worksheets and are not looking at you. You can use any audible method to produce the signal—clapping, finger snapping, or tapping your book.

1. Ask the question.
2. Pause one second.
3. Tap. Students should respond immediately after the tap. (In place of the tap any audible signal is acceptable.)

EXERCISE 2

Place Value: Introducing Hundreds Number

a. Find Part 2 on your worksheet. ✔

b. These are hundreds numbers. Hundreds numbers have three digits.

c. I'll read the first hundreds number. You read the rest of them.

d. Item A is two hundred sixty-four.

e. Everybody, read item B. (Signal.) *Five hundred thirty-eight.*

- Read item C. (Signal.) *Four hundred ninety.*
- Read item D. (Signal.) *Seven hundred fifty-one.*
- Read item E. (Signal.) *Eight hundred ninety-two.*
- Read item F. (Signal.) *Three hundred seventy-six.*
- (Repeat step e until firm.)

f. (Call on individual students. Each student is to read all the numbers in Part 2.)

The Point-Touch Signal This signal is used when pointing to facts, problems, or symbols that are written on the board. The following exercise is from *Multiplication,* Lesson 10. In this exercise, you write a list of multiplication facts on the board (or on an overhead transparency). After the students read each fact in the list, you erase the facts, and the students practice recalling the facts.

EXERCISE 1

Facts: Introducing Three Facts in Series

a. (Write on the board:)

$$9 \times 1 = 9$$
$$9 \times 2 = 18$$
$$9 \times 3 = 27$$

b. These are facts that start with 9. Let's read the facts together, starting with 9 times 1. Get ready. (Read the facts with the students. Signal.) *9 times 1 equals 9; 9 times 2 equals 18; 9 times 3 equals 27.*

In step b, the teacher and students are reading the facts together.

To execute the point-touch signal in step b:

1. Hold your finger about an inch away from the board, pointing to the beginning of the first fact. Be careful not to cover any part of the fact or obscure it from any student's view.

2. As you point, say Get ready.

3. Pause 1 second.

4. Signal by tapping in front of the fact. Students should respond the instant you signal (touch the board).

Corrections

All students will make mistakes. These mistakes provide you with valuable information about the difficulties the students are having. Knowing how to correct effectively is essential to successful teaching.

- Correct all mistakes immediately.
- Correct the entire group even though only some students may be having difficulty. This practice provides more instruction and prevents other students from making similar errors.
- Use quick pacing, and demonstrate an upbeat, positive attitude when correcting.
- Praise students when you do not have to correct them, particularly on difficult items.

Two kinds of correction procedures are used in *Corrective Mathematics*—general corrections and specific corrections.

General Corrections

To achieve mastery, all students must respond at the same time. That way, all students are engaged, you can hear errors, and you can tell when a student isn't participating.

If a student fails to answer when you give the signal, correct by saying:

- I have to hear everybody. Let's try it again.
- Then return to the beginning of the exercise.

If a student responds either before or too long after your signal, call attention to the signal, and return to the beginning of the exercise. For example, if students respond before you signal, say:

- You have to wait until I signal. Let's try it again.
- Then return to the beginning of the exercise.

Specific Corrections

Corrections are the primary tool used for diagnostic/prescriptive teaching. Through mistakes, students indicate what they don't know. The type of error indicates whether students need practice in recalling specific information or applying a process.

When students don't know the correct answer to a question you present, correct with the following steps:

1. **(Model)** Stop the students by saying Listen or My turn. Then tell them the answer.

2. **(Test)** Repeat the step. Repeat the instructions you gave the students, and have them respond to the task they missed.

3. **(Delayed Test)** Provide a delayed test by returning to the beginning of the exercise in which the mistake occurred and presenting the steps in order.

4. To correct persistent mistakes, present similar exercises, which usually can be found in earlier lessons.

Correction 1 You can use the **model-test correction** to correct errors students make when they are asked to recall specific information, such as arithmetic facts. Your correction consists of telling students the correct answer and then testing them to make sure they can answer correctly.

Follow these steps when correcting the students:

1. **(Model)** Tell students the correct answer.

2. **(Test)** Check to make sure they respond correctly.

3. **(Delayed Test)** Return to the beginning of the exercise to determine if their response is firm.

Example: Students make a mistake in step c of *Addition,* Lesson 2, Exercise 6.

▶ **EXERCISE 6**

Place Value: Practice Reading Hundreds Numbers

a. Find Part 4 on your worksheet. ✔
b. Read item A. Get ready. (Signal.) *Two hundred seventy-nine.*
- What digit is in the hundreds column? (Signal.) *2.*
- What digit is in the tens column? (Signal.) *7.*
- What digit is in the ones column? (Signal.) *9.*
c. Read item B. Get ready. (Signal.) *One hundred forty-six.*
- What digit is in the hundreds column? (Signal.) *6.*

Correction

Stop the students as soon as a mistake occurs.

---

1. **(Model)** Listen: One hundred forty-six.
- My turn. What digit is in the hundreds column? 1.
2. **(Test)** Read item B again. Get ready. (Signal.) *One hundred forty-six.*
- What digit is in the hundreds column? (Signal.) *1.*
- What digit is in the tens column? (Signal.) *4.*
- What digit is in the ones column? (Signal.) *6.*
3. **(Delayed Test)** Read item A. Get ready. (Signal) *Two hundred seventy-nine.*
- What digit is in the hundreds column? (Signal.) *2.*
- What digit is in the tens column? (Signal.) *7.*
- What digit is in the ones column? (Signal.) *9.*
- Read item B. Get ready. (Signal.) *One hundred forty-six.*

- What digit is in the hundreds column? (Signal) *1.*
- What digit is in the tens column? (Signal.) *4.*
- What digit is in the ones column? (Signal.) *6.*

Workbook Reference

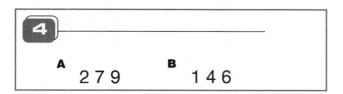

Correction 2 The **model-lead-test correction** is used when a response is difficult for students to produce. These responses usually involve students reading problems or repeating rules. Errors occur because students have difficulty saying all the words in the right order. Your correction consists of telling students the correct answer, then leading the students through the response by responding with them, and finally testing students to make sure they can answer correctly. When the students respond correctly on the test, you provide a delayed test.

Follow these steps when correcting students:

1. **(Model)** Tell students the correct answer.
2. **(Lead)** Say the response with the students. You may need to repeat this step three to five times.
3. **(Test)** Check to make sure students respond correctly.
4. **(Delayed Test)** Return to the beginning of the exercise to determine if their response is firm.

Example: Students do not say the subtraction fact in *Subtraction,* Lesson 11, Exercise 8, step c.

▶ EXERCISE 8

Facts: Practicing Number Families

a. Find Part 5 of your worksheet. ✔
b. Look at number family A. The two small numbers are 1 and 6. So what's the big number? (Signal.) *7.*
- Write the big number in the box. ✔
c. Say the subtraction fact that minuses 1. (Signal.) *1 minus.*

Workbook Reference

A
$\left\{\begin{array}{l} 1 \text{ ----------------------} \\ \\ 6 \text{ ----------------------} \end{array}\right.$

Correction

Stop the students as soon as the mistake occurs.

1. **(Model)** Listen. 7 minus 1 equals 6.
2. **(Lead)** Say it with me. (Signal and respond with the students.) *7 minus 1 equals 6.*
3. **(Test)** Your turn. Say the subtraction fact that minuses 1. (Signal.) *7 minus 1 equals 6.*
- Say the subtraction fact that minuses 6. (Signal.) *7 minus 6 equals 1.*
4. **(Delayed Test)** Starting over.
- Look at number family A. The two small numbers are 1 and 6. So what's the big number? (Signal.) *7.*
- Say the subtraction fact that minuses 1. (Signal.) *7 minus 1 equals 6.*
- Say the subtraction fact that minuses 6. (Signal.) *7 minus 6 equals 1.*

Correction 3 The **process correction** is used in situations in which students have to apply rules or procedures in their heads in order to produce the correct response. When you use a process correction, you guide the students through the steps they learned in earlier exercises. Your correction consists of telling students the correct answer, then leading the students through the response by asking a series of questions that make the process overt, and finally testing students to make sure they can answer correctly. When the students respond correctly on the test, you provide a delayed test.

Follow these steps when correcting the students:

1. **(Model)** Tell students the rule.

2. **(Lead)** Present a series of questions that make the process overt. The questions you use will change depending on the mistake and the skills that have been presented previously. However, it is always based on skills taught in earlier lessons so it is easy for you to present.

3. **(Test)** Check to make sure students respond correctly.

4. **(Delayed Test)** Return to the beginning of the exercise to determine if their response is firm.

Example: In the *Subtraction* module, the students learn this rule about number families: If the big number is given, you write a subtraction problem. If the big number is **not** given, you write an addition problem. They have also had heavily prompted practice in determining which operation to perform—addition or subtraction.

In this example from *Subtraction,* Lesson 29, Exercise 6, students chose the wrong operation, subtracting instead of adding in the second problem.

> ▶ **EXERCISE 6**
>
> ## Story Problems: Rules for Adding and Subtracting
>
> a. (Continue with worksheet Part 5.) Touch number family A again. ✔
> - Is the big number given? (Signal.) *Yes.*
> - So what kind of problem are you going to write? (Signal.) *Subtraction.*

b. I'll say the problem without the answer. 9 minus 4 equals how many? Say the problem. (Signal.) *9 minus 4 equals how many?*

c. Write the problem and draw a box for how many. ✔

New Problem

a. Touch number family B. ✔
- Is the big number given? (Signal.) *No.*
- So what kind of problem are you going to write? (Signal.) *Subtraction.*

Workbook Reference

Part 5
A
The big number is 9. A small number is 4

B
The small number is 10. Another small number is 4

Correction

Stop the students as soon as the mistake occurs.

1. **(Model)** Listen. Addition.

2. (**Lead** by repeating the rule, followed by a series of questions that prompt students to remember the rule. Use questions similar to those presented in earlier exercises.)
- If the big number is given, you write a subtraction problem. If the big number is **not** given, you write an addition problem.
- What kind of problem do you write if the big number is given? (Signal.) *Subtraction.*
- What kind of problem do you write if the big number is not given? (Signal.) *Addition.*
- If the big number is **not** given in a number family, you write an addition problem.

3. **(Test)** Look at number family B again. Is the big number given? (Signal.) *No.*

- So what kind of problem do you write? (Signal.) *Addition.*
- I'll say the problem without the answer. 10 plus 4 equals how many? Say the problem. (Signal.) *10 plus 4 equals how many?*
- Write the problem and draw a box for how many. ✔

4. **(Delayed Test)** Starting over. Look at number family A again.
- Is the big number given? (Signal.) *Yes.*
- So what kind of problem are you going to write? (Signal.) *Subtraction.*
- I'll say the problem without the answer. 9 minus 4 equals how many? Say the problem. (Signal.) *9 minus 4 equals how many?*

New Problem

a. Touch number family B.
- Is the big number given? (Signal.) *No.*
- So what kind of problem do you write? (Signal.) *Addition.*
b. Say the problem without the answer. (Signal.) *10 minus 4 equals how many?*

Teaching to Criterion

At the conclusion of any exercise, each student should be able to respond without making any mistakes. Your goal as a teacher should be to see that students are "firm"—that is, meet this criterion.

Let students know what you expect from them. Keep on an exercise until you can honestly say to them, Great! Everybody answered every question correctly.

If your criterion for an exercise is strict, the group will have less difficulty with similar exercises in subsequent lessons.

The instruction "Repeat until firm" that appears in many exercises indicates that certain steps should be taught to criterion. Although the instruction to repeat until firm does not appear in every exercise, you should be sure to correct and then repeat steps on which errors are made.

Individual Turns

Individual turns are incorporated into many exercises. You should think of individual turns as part of your goal of teaching to criterion. Are you positive, after presenting a particular exercise, that every student can perform every step? If not, present individual turns. Present turns frequently enough that students get the idea that they are individually accountable for the information. About half of the individual turns should be presented to the lowest-performing students in the group. The remainder should be distributed among the other students.

If a student makes a mistake on an individual turn, avoid correcting only that student. Present the correction to the entire group. After testing the entire group, present the question that was missed to the student who missed it. This procedure is efficient because if one student fails an individual turn, others in the group usually will make the same mistake on that exercise. By correcting the group, you are in effect correcting in advance the mistakes the other students might make.

Worksheets

During each lesson, a skill will first be taught or reviewed on the board, and then the students will do similar problems on their worksheets. This procedure will be repeated several times during each lesson. Make sure the students do not go ahead and work other problems.

If only a few students do not finish a section in a reasonable time, go on with the next exercise. Later in the day, give those students who did not finish enough time to complete each section. If this is a persistent occurrence, you might want to do the previous lesson's workcheck at the beginning of the period so all students may grade their worksheets at the same time.

Workchecks

At the end of each lesson is a workcheck. In the *Addition, Subtraction, Multiplication,* and *Division* modules, the students check their own Workbooks and correct their mistakes. In the other modules, students exchange Workbooks during workchecks. Walk around the room during the workcheck to make sure that everybody is marking wrong answers.

After the students have finished checking their Workbooks, they will fill out their charts. They also complete five-lesson point graphs. During the first few lessons, help the students through the procedure for recording errors, determining points, and totaling points. After the first three days, it should not be necessary to help the students complete their charts. However, it is a good idea to occasionally collect student Workbooks and check to make sure that the students are giving themselves the correct number of points.

Diagnosing Worksheet Errors

If a student makes more than an occasional error (consistently fails to earn points for the worksheet), treat this as an indication that the student needs help. In order to provide this help, you must analyze the student's worksheet errors.

If the student's errors do not follow any particular pattern, the student is probably being careless. To reduce the number of careless errors, examine the use of points and praise during the lesson, and adjust the management system so the student will be more highly motivated to be careful.

If the student's errors follow a pattern, the pattern is likely to fall into one of two categories.

Sometimes an error pattern reveals fact deficiency. A student might make many errors on the fact section of the worksheets or might make fact errors on computational or story problem sections of the worksheets. For instance, a student might make this error:

$$
\begin{array}{r}
95 \\
7\overline{)595} \\
-56 \\
\hline
35 \\
-35 \\
\hline
0
\end{array}
$$

The student did all the steps in the division process correctly but confused two facts: 7×8 and 7×9.

When students consistently make fact errors, provide additional practice on those facts. When providing additional practice, make it entertaining; for instance, use contests between teams or challenges. Make sure students are not using their fingers during fact practices, perhaps giving bonus points for not using fingers or decreasing the amount of time students have to do a series of facts.

Sometimes student errors indicate a process deficiency.

$$
\begin{array}{r}
^{8} \\
32 \\
\times \quad 9 \\
\hline
351
\end{array}
$$

In this problem, the student carried the wrong number. If the student makes more than an occasional error of this type, work with the student using a process correction. Rewrite the problem on a clean sheet of paper. Then, guide the student through the problem, paying particular attention to the part of the process in which the student made the error. In this example, you might say:

- What numbers do you multiply first?
- What's the answer?
- Yes, the answer is 18. Remember, you carry the 1 to the tens column, and you write the 8 in the ones column. Which digit do you carry to the tens column?
- Write the 1 above the tens column.
- Which digit do you write in the ones column?
- Do it.

To ensure that the student is firm on the problem part of the process, write several additional problems of the same type, and guide the student through the problems. Pay particular attention to the part of the process with which the student is having difficulty. When the student seems firm, have the student work a few problems independently. If the student is successful, the problem has probably been remediated.

Errors on story problems might also indicate one or two process deficiencies. One type of process deficiency occurs in computation—performing the operation called for. The other deficiency involves translating the words into the appropriate numerical statements.

If a student consistently writes the wrong sign when translating a story problem into a numerical statement, present a series of story problems, and guide the student through the discrimination process. For instance, in the *Subtraction* module you might say:

- Read this story problem.
- Is the big number given?
- So is it an addition or a subtraction problem?

After the student seems firm, have the student work a few problems independently. If the student is successful, the problem has probably been remediated.

If students confuse multiplication and division story problems, you might need to be more specific in correcting errors. You might say, for instance:

- Read the sentence that has **each** (or **every**) to yourself, and find the word that tells about the big number.
- What word tells about the big number?
- Read the entire problem and get ready to tell me whether the big number is given.
- So do you multiply or divide?

Some students might make story problem errors because of decoding or language deficits. Read and explain any unfamiliar vocabulary until such time as the students can proceed without this help. Read story problems to students who have serious problems with decoding.

General Motivation

The single most powerful factor that influences student enthusiasm for the program is *teacher* enthusiasm. Remember, if you are excited about the program, your students will reflect that excitement.

The best way for you to achieve and maintain enthusiasm is to periodically take stock of student achievement in the program. Praise students for hard work, and keep reminding them of the importance of the skills they are learning. Recognize the progress they are making.

Praise

Praising students when they do well is a good way to help them understand exactly what kind of performance you expect. Praise will also keep students highly motivated. Following these guidelines will help make praise effective:

- Early in the program praise students who get to their seats on time, quickly open their Workbooks to the right page, or otherwise demonstrate their readiness to learn. Soon shift emphasis, however, and begin concentrating on praising good mathematics performance.
- Be especially careful to pay positive attention when the group shows improvement on a task that has presented difficulty in the past or when a student is working hard without having immediate success. Encourage students to put out the effort necessary for success with praise statements such as Great. Today everyone remembered how to do that problem. I'm really proud of you or That's a difficult problem to solve, Matthew, but you're getting better. If you keep working at it, you're going to get it down perfectly.
- The more specific the praise, the more effective it will be. You worked every problem on your worksheet right. Terrific! will work better than Good job.

Awarding Points

Corrective Mathematics includes a point system designed to turn mathematics instruction into a positive experience for students. The top of the first page of each lesson in the Workbook displays one of more boxes for recording the number of points earned.

Points are primarily designed for accurate Workbook performance on the teacher-directed and Independent Work sections. A schedule for awarding points is provided in each Teacher Presentation Book. Students record points in boxes depending on the activities involved.

On the inside back cover of the Workbook are the Point Summary Charts. A sample is shown below. These charts are designed to show a student's performance for each block of five lessons.

- After computing the total points for a lesson, the student records the daily total in the appropriate lesson box.
- After every fifth lesson, the student adds the total points earned for the five-lesson segment and records the total in the box headed "Total."

Lesson	1	2	3	4	5	Total
Points						

Such charts are important for two reasons. First, they show students their own progress. Second, points may be used as a basis for giving students grades indicating their overall level of achievement.

Preparing to Teach a Lesson

In order to teach a *Corrective Mathematics* lesson effectively, you must be able to present the lesson accurately, adhering closely to the words of the script. You should be able to present the lesson at a relatively rapid rate to ensure the students' attention. You should be able to do these things without looking at the script too frequently, because failure to watch the students closely usually leads to unnoticed and, consequently, uncorrected errors.

The most efficient way to prepare to teach a lesson is to look through the script and identify the new formats. These are the only formats that will require attention. Examine each new format and answer six questions:

- What is this format teaching?
- How is it structured?
- Does the format specify that any steps are to be repeated?
- Where are individual turns specified?
- What kinds of mistakes are students likely to make?
- What correction procedure should be used?

Look through the Guide section of the Teacher's Presentation Book to see whether it includes a sample of the new format exercise. If it does, read the accompanying information carefully. Then practice presenting the exercise, using signals, repeating steps as specified, giving individual turns, and practicing corrections. Continue practicing until you can present the exercise at a relatively rapid rate, referring to the script only occasionally. Practice the script aloud. If possible, another adult should play the role of the student.

Self-Evaluation

When beginning *Corrective Mathematics* instructions, you will benefit from a brief self-evaluation after each lesson. Later in the year, you may conduct self-evaluations less often, perhaps every week or two.

When evaluating your instruction, ask yourself whether you have adhered to the guidelines presented in the Teaching Strategies section of this guide (pages 37–47). If you feel that you have, for instance, failed to pace the lesson rapidly enough or failed to follow the script closely, concentrate on pacing or script presentation in subsequent lessons until these skills are automatic.

Using the following self-evaluation form might make this process easier.

		Yes	No
1. Formats	I am following the format closely enough to ensure consistent and careful instruction.		
2. Signals	All my students are responding together and when I want them to.		
3. Watching	I am always paying close attention to my students. When they are writing or checking written work, I'm walking among them.		
4. Corrections	I am correcting every error. My students know that when I make a correction, I'm really helping them improve.		
5. Feedback	My students always know when they are doing a good job. My comments are sincere.		
6. Pacing	I am going through the lessons as fast as I can without forcing the students to make mistakes.		
7. Success	I can justify working this hard because my students are experiencing success.		

Teacher Practice Formats

This section contains a group of formats that you should master before you begin teaching *Corrective Mathematics*. Ideally, the analysis and practice of these formats will take place in a training session conducted by an experienced trainer. If you cannot attend a training session about the *Corrective Mathematics* series, you should study the accompanying information carefully and practice the formats aloud.

The following formats are grouped according to whether they teach facts, operations, or story problems. Mastery of these formats is an essential first step in teaching *Corrective Mathematics* effectively. It does not, however, substitute for ongoing mastery of the new formats that appear in each lesson. The formats on the following pages should be mastered before beginning instruction.

Facts

Format 1:
Addition, Lesson 2, EXERCISE 3

EXERCISE 3

Facts: Introducing Number Families

a. Find Part 3 on your worksheet. ✔
b. These are number families for addition. A number family is made up of two small numbers and a big number. The small numbers are inside the bracket of the number family. The big number is in the box.
c. Look at number family A. (Pause.) What's the big number? (Signal.) *7.*
 • That's the number you end up with when you add the two small numbers in the family.
 • What are the two small numbers in the family? (Signal.) *6 and 1.*
d. Here's an addition fact using the numbers in family A. 6 plus 1 equals 7. Say that fact. (Signal.) *6 plus 1 equals 7.*
e. Here's another addition fact for family A. 1 plus 6 equals 7. Say that fact. (Signal.) *1 plus 6 equals 7.*
f. (Repeat steps d and e until firm.)

Workbook

$$A \quad \boxed{7} \left\{ \begin{array}{l} 6 \quad \underline{\;6+1=7\;} \; \text{-----} \\ \\ 1 \quad \underline{\;1+6=7\;} \; \text{-----} \end{array} \right.$$

What is this format teaching? This format is teaching number-family conventions (the small numbers are inside the bracket; the big number is in the box) and the procedures for translating a number family into two addition facts.

How is it structured? You explain "number families," "small numbers," and "big numbers." The students apply this information to the number family on the worksheet. You then say the two addition facts that derive from the number family, and the students repeat the facts.

Does the format specify that any steps are to be repeated? Step f requires that steps d and e be repeated until the students can say the facts firmly.

Where are individual turns specified? Individual turns are not specified in this format, but you can present steps d and e to individuals after the group has practiced saying the facts.

What kinds of mistakes are the students likely to make, and what correction procedures should be used? The students might say "6" for the first response in step c. You should use a process correction.

 • Listen. The big number is in the **box.** Read the number that is in the **box.** (Signal.) *7.*
 • So what's the big number? (Signal.) *7.*

Students might have trouble saying the facts in steps d and e. If so, use the model-lead-test correction.

 • Listen. 1 plus 6 equals 7.
 • Say it with me. 1 plus 6 equals 7.
 • Your turn. Say the fact. (Signal.) *1 plus 6 equals 7.*

Format 2:
Subtraction, Lesson 17, EXERCISE 4

Prior to Lesson 17, the students have worked with number families in which all three numbers are given and with number families in which the students have to find the big number. The students have learned how to identify the "big number" and the "small numbers," how to translate a number family into addition and subtraction facts, and how to find a missing big number by adding the two small numbers.

EXERCISE 4

Facts: Number Families—Small Number Missing

a. Find Part 3 on your worksheet.
b. In these number families, the big number and one small number are given. You have to find the other small number.

---

c. Here's a rule. If a number family gives the big number and one small number, you have to subtract to find the other small number. If the big number is given, what do you do to find the other small number? (Signal.) *Subtract.*

d. Look at number family A. What's the big number? (Signal.) *12.*
- What's the small number? (Signal.) *5.*

e. My turn. What problem do you have to work to find the missing small number? (Pause.) 12 minus 5. Your turn. What problem do you have to work? (Signal.) *12 minus 5.*

f. What's 12 minus 5? (Signal.) *7.*
- Write 7 in the box. ✔

g. Now you're going to say both subtraction facts. First say the fact that minuses 5. (Signal.) *12 minus 5 equals 7.*
- Say the fact that minuses 7. (Signal.) *12 minus 7 equals 5.*

h. Now write the two subtraction facts. ✔

i. Do the rest of the number families in Part 3 on your own. First figure out the missing small number. Then write the two subtraction facts.
- (Check and correct.)

j. Let's check your work. Put an **X** next to each problem you got wrong.

k. Number family B. What's the missing small number? (Signal.) *8.*
- Say the subtraction fact that minuses 4. (Signal.) *12 minus 4 equals 8.*
- Say the subtraction fact that minuses 8. (Signal.) *12 minus 8 equals 4.*

l. Number family C. What's the missing small number? (Signal.) *9.*
- Say the subtraction fact that minuses 3. (Signal.) *12 minus 3 equals 9.*
- Say the subtraction fact that minuses 9. (Signal.) *12 minus 9 equals 3.*

m. Number family D. What's the missing small number? (Signal.) *10.*
- Say the subtraction fact that minuses 2. (Signal.) *12 minus 2 equals 10.*
- Say the subtraction fact that minuses 10. (Signal.) *12 minus 10 equals 2.*

Workbook

What is the format teaching? This format is teaching the students how to find a missing small number in a number family.

How is it structured? You give the rule for finding a missing small number, quiz the students on the rule, and help them apply the rule to problem A. When the students know the missing small number, they say and write the two subtraction facts that derive from the number family. The students work the remaining three problems independently, and then you help the students check their work.

Does the format specify that any steps are to be repeated? No.

Where are individual turns specified? Individual turns are not specified for this format. The students' written performance on problems B through D should be a sufficient check of individual mastery.

What kinds of mistakes are the students likely to make, and what correction procedures should be used? The students might give the wrong response at step f. Use a model-test correction.

- Listen. Seven.
- What's 12 minus 5? (Signal.) *7.*

The students might have trouble saying the facts in step g or in steps k through m. Use a model-lead-test correction.

- Listen. The subtraction fact that minuses 4 is 12 minus 4 equals 8. 12 minus 4 equals 8.
- Say it with me. 12 minus 4 equals 8.
- Your turn. Say the fact. (Signal.) *12 minus 4 equals 8.*

The students might write the wrong numbers in the boxes for problems B through D, adding instead of subtracting. Use a process correction.

- If a number family gives the big number and one small number, you have to subtract to find the other small number.
- Does the number family in problem B give the big number and one small number? (Signal.) *Yes.*
- So what do you have to do to find the other small number? (Signal.) *Subtract.*
- What problem do you have to work? (Signal.) *12 minus 4.*
- What's the answer? (Signal.) *8.*
- So what's the missing small number? (Signal.) *8.*

Format 3:
Multiplication, Lesson 1, EXERCISE 4

EXERCISE 4

Facts: Introducing Number Families

a. There are number families for multiplication. Each family is made up of three numbers that always go together when you multiply. There are two small numbers and a big number.

b. The number families that you use for addition and subtraction are not the same number families that you use for multiplication.

c. Find Part 4 on your worksheet. ✔

d. Touch number family A. The numbers inside the bracket are the small numbers. I'll tell you the small numbers in family A. 10 and 9.

e. When you multiply the two small numbers, you end up with 90. That's the big number. Write 90 in the box. ✔

f. We can make two multiplication facts from number family A. Here's the first fact. 10 times 9 equals 90. Say it. (Signal.) *10 times 9 equals 90.*
- Here's the other fact. 9 times 10 equals 90. Say it. (Signal.) *9 times 10 equals 90.*

g. Write both facts below number family A. ✔

Workbook

What is this format teaching? This format is teaching the conventions of multiplication number families: the small numbers are inside the bracket; the big number is in the box. It is also teaching how to find a missing big number and the procedures for translating the number family into multiplication facts.

How is it structured? You explain "number families," "small numbers," "big numbers," and how to find a missing big number. You then say the two multiplication facts that derive from the number family, and the students repeat and write the facts.

Does the format specify that any steps are to be repeated? No.

Where are individual turns specified? Individual turns are not specified for this format. The students' written performance should be a sufficient check of individual mastery.

What kinds of mistakes are the students likely to make, and what correction procedures should be used? The students might have difficulty saying the facts in step f. Use a model-lead-test correction procedure.

- Listen again. 10 times 9 equals 90.
- Say it with me. 10 times 9 equals 90.
- Your turn. Say the fact. (Signal.) *10 times 9 equals 90.*

Format 4:
Division, **Lesson 2, EXERCISE 4**

In Lesson 1, the students worked with number families in which all three numbers are given and with number families with a missing small number. The students have learned what the terms "big number" and "small number" mean and how to translate a number family into multiplication and division facts.

EXERCISE 4

Fact Number Families:
Multiplication and Division Facts

a. Find Part 4 on your worksheet. ✔

b. First you're going to say two multiplication facts for each number family. Then you're going to write two division facts for that family.

c. Say the multiplication fact for number family A that starts with 5. Get ready. (Signal.) *5 times 4 equals 20.*
- Say the other fact for number family A. Get ready. (Signal.) *4 times 5 equals 20.*

d. What is the big number for number family A? (Signal.) *20.*
- Remember, when you write the division fact, the big number goes below the sign. One small number goes before the sign. The answer goes above the last digit of 20.

e. Write both division facts for number family A. ✔

$$5\overline{)20}^{\,4} \qquad 4\overline{)20}^{\,5}$$

f. Touch number family B. ✔
- Say the multiplication fact for number family B that starts with 9. (Signal.) *9 times 4 equals 36.*
- Say the other multiplication fact for number family B. (Signal.) *4 times 9 equals 36.*

g. What's the big number for number family B? (Signal.) *36.*
- Write both division facts for number family B. ✔

$$9\overline{)36}^{\,4} \qquad 4\overline{)36}^{\,9}$$

h. (Repeat steps f and g for number families C and D.)

Workbook

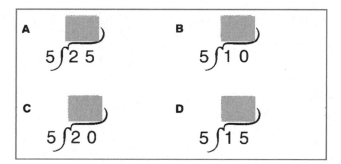

What is this format teaching? This format reviews and gives the student practice using a number family to generate two division facts.

How is it structured? The students say the two multiplication facts that derive from the number family in problem A, and they identify the big number. You review the procedure for writing division facts, and the students write the division facts that derive from the number family. These steps are repeated in abbreviated form for each of the three remaining problems.

Does the format specify that any steps are to be repeated? Step h requires that steps f and g are to be repeated with number families C and D.

Where are individual turns specified? Individual turns are not specified for this format. The students' written performance on problems B through D should be a sufficient check of individual mastery.

What kinds of mistakes are the students likely to make, and what correction procedures should be used? The students might have difficulty saying the facts in steps c and f. Use the model-lead-test correction procedure.

- Listen. The multiplication fact for number family B that starts with 9 is 9 times 4 equals 36.
- Say it with me. 9 times 4 equals 36.
- Your turn. Say the fact. (Signal.) *9 times 4 equals 36.*

The students might say one of the small numbers for the first response in step d or g. Use a process correction. The following refers to a rule students learned earlier: "The big number is outside the bracket."

- Listen. The big number is **outside the bracket.** Which number is **outside the bracket?** (Signal.) *20.*
- So what's the big number? (Signal.) *20.*

The students might fail to write the answer above the last digit of the big number when writing the facts in steps d and g. Use a process correction.

- Remember, when you write the division fact, you write the answer above the last digit of the big number. What's the last number of the big number? (Signal.) *6.*
- Erase your answer, and write it above the last digit.

Operations

Format 5:
Addition, Lesson 28, **EXERCISE 8**

Prior to Lesson 28, the students worked addition problems with three or more single-digit numbers and multicolumn problems that do not require carrying. The students learned to compute silently (to add numbers that aren't written), to start with the ones column when working a column problem, to write an answer in the hundreds column when the tens column sum in a 2-column problem exceeds 9 tens, and to identify the number of tens in a 2-digit number.

EXERCISE 8

Operations: Introducing **Renaming the Ones Column**

a. Find Part 7 on your worksheet.
b. Touch problem A. ✔
- I'll read the ones column. 9 plus 9 plus 2 plus 5. The answer for the ones column is written in the circle next to the problem. What is the answer for the ones column? (Signal.) *25.*

---

c. Touch problem B. ✔
- I'll read the ones column. 9 plus 5 plus 6 plus 3. The answer for the ones column is written in the circle next to the problem. What is the answer for the ones column? (Signal.) *23.*
d. Touch problem C. I'll read the ones column. 3 plus 2 plus 5 plus 4. What is the answer for the ones column? (Signal.) *14.*
e. Touch problem D. I'll read the ones column. 9 plus 9 plus 9 plus 5. What is the answer for the ones column? (Signal.) *32.*
f. In each of these problems, the answer for the ones column is more than 9. When the answer for the ones column is more than 9, you have to carry the tens number to the tens column.
g. Look at problem A. The answer for the ones column is 25. How many tens are in 25? (Signal.) *2.*
- So how many tens do you carry to the tens column? (Signal.) *2.*
h. Look at problem B. The answer for the ones column is 23. How many tens are in 23? (Signal.) *2.*
- So how many tens do you carry to the tens column? (Signal.) *2.*
i. Look at problem C. The answer for the ones column is 14. How many tens are in 14? (Signal.) *1.*
- So how many tens do you carry to the tens column? (Signal.) *1.*
j. Look at problem D. The answer for the ones column is 32. How many tens are in 32? (Signal.) *3.*
- So how many tens do you carry to the tens column? (Signal.) *3.*
k. Now we're going to work the problems.
l. Look at problem A again. The answer for the ones column is 25. Write the 5 in the ones column. ✔
m. How many tens are in 25? (Signal.) *2.*
- So you must carry the 2 tens to the tens column. Write a 2 in the box at the top of the tens column. (Pause.)
n. Now add the tens column. Start with the 2 tens you carried. (Pause.) What's the answer for the tens column? (Signal.) *9 tens.*
- So the answer for the problem is 95.

Workbook

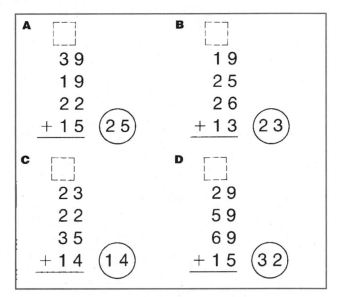

What is this format teaching? This format combines all of the preskills and teaches the entire procedure for carrying from the ones column to the tens column.

How is it structured? You read the ones column for each of a series of problems in which the ones-column answer is already provided. The students read the answers for the ones columns. You point out that each of the answers is more than 9 and explain the carrying procedure. For each of the problems, the students identify the number of tens that have to be carried to the tens column. Then you help the students apply the procedure to problem A.

Does the format specify that any steps are to be repeated? No.

Where are individual turns specified? Individual turns are not specified for this format. The students' written performance in steps l through j can be used for individuals after the group has been firmed.

What kinds of mistakes are the students likely to make, and what correction procedures should be used? The students might give the wrong answer in step n. You could use a process correction that involves a procedure presented earlier for silent computation.

- Read the first two numbers in the tens column. (Signal.) *2 and 3.*
- What's 2 plus 3? (Signal.) *5.*
- Your turn. Say the fact. (Signal.) *2 plus 3 equals 5.*
- Read the next number in the tens column. (Signal.) *1.*
- Add it to 5, and tell me the answer. (Signal.) *6.*
- Read the next number in the tens column. (Signal.) *2.*
- Add it to 6, and tell me the answer. (Signal.) *8.*
- Read the next number. (Signal.) *1.*
- Add it to 8, and tell me the answer. (Signal.) *9.*
- So what's the answer for the tens column? (Signal.) *9.*

Format 6:
Subtraction, **Lesson 18, EXERCISE 6**

Prior to Lesson 18, the students worked subtraction problems with multidigit numbers and no borrowing. The students learned to start with the ones column when subtracting multidigit numbers, to rewrite numbers by borrowing, to determine when borrowing is necessary, and to subtract when the borrowing has been done.

EXERCISE 6

Operations: Doing All Steps in a Borrowing Problem

a. Find Part 6 on your worksheet.
b. You'll have to borrow in each of these problems. Problem A. 396 minus 248. Read the problem in the ones column. (Signal.) *6 minus 8.*
c. Do you have to borrow? (Signal.) *Yes.*
- Which digit do you borrow from? (Signal.) *9.*
d. Slash the 9. How many will be left? (Signal.) *8.*
- Do the borrowing and write the numbers where they belong. ✔
e. Read the new problem in the ones column. (Signal.) *16 minus 8.*
- Read the new problem in the tens column. (Signal.) *8 minus 4.*
- Read the problem in the hundreds column. (Signal.) *3 minus 2.*

Workbook

A
$$\begin{array}{r} \overset{8}{3}\overset{1}{\cancel{9}}6 \\ -248 \\ \hline 148 \end{array}$$

B
$$\begin{array}{r} \overset{5}{\cancel{6}}\overset{1}{0}7 \\ -497 \\ \hline 110 \end{array}$$

What's this format teaching? This format combines all of the previously presented preskills and teaches the entire procedure for working problems that involve borrowing from one column.

How is it structured? The students read the problem in the ones column of problem A, decide that they have to borrow, do the borrowing, read the new problem in each column, and then figure out the answer to problem A. This procedure is repeated for problem B. In problem B, however, the problem in the tens column requires borrowing.

Does the format specify that any steps are to be repeated? No.

Where are individual turns specified? Individual turns are not specified for this format. The students' written performance should provide a sufficient check of individual mastery.

What kinds of mistakes are the students likely to make, and what correction procedures should be used? The students might say "no" as the answer in the first step c. Use a process correction.

- Read the problem in the ones column again. (Signal.) *6 minus 8.*
- How many are you starting with? (Signal.) *6.*
- Are you minusing more than you start with? (Signal.) *Yes.*
- So do you have to borrow? (Signal.) *Yes.*

The students might give the wrong answer in step f. If the borrowing was done improperly, the students should erase their work, and you should take them through steps b through f again. This constitutes a process correction. If the borrowing was done properly and a fact error was made, use a model-test correction. For example, if the student wrote 147 as the

answer to the problem 396 − 248, you would use a model-test correction for the mistake made in the ones column.

Format 7:
Multiplication, Lesson 17, EXERCISE 7

Prior to Lesson 17, the students worked non-carrying column problems involving 2-digit or 3-digit numbers times 1-digit numbers. The students learned to read the problems from bottom to top ($\begin{array}{r}41\\ \times\ 2\end{array}$ is read "41 times 2," and the relevant subproblems are read "2 times 1" and "2 times 4"). The students also learned to start multiplying in the ones column and to write the digits in the answer below the appropriate digits in the problem.

EXERCISE 7

Operations: Introducing Multidigit Times Single-Digit Numbers—With Carrying

a. Find Part 6 on your worksheet.
- You have to carry to work these problems.

b. I'll read problem A. 14 times 5. First you're going to multiply the number in the ones column. Then you're going to multiply the number in the tens column.

c. Say the problem and the answer for multiplying the number in the ones column. (Pause.) Get ready. (Signal.) *5 times 4 equals 20.*

d. When you multiply the ones column, the answer is 20. You have to carry the 2 to the tens column and you write the 0 in the ones column.

e. Touch the dotted 2 that is carried to the tens column. ✔
- Touch the dotted 0 in the ones column. ✔
- Trace the dotted 2 and 0.

f. I'll say the problem for multiplying the number in the tens column. 5 times 1. Say the problem and the answer for multiplying the number in the tens column. (Signal.) *5 times 1 equals 5.*

g. Now add the 2 you carried to 5. What does 5 plus 2 equal? (Signal.) *7.*
- Trace the dotted 7.

Workbook

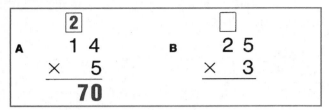

What is this format teaching? This format combines all previously discussed preskills and teaches the entire process of working 2-digit times 1-digit problems that involve carrying.

How is it structured? You read problem A and guide the students through multiplying in the ones column, carrying, multiplying in the tens column, and adding the carried number. You then guide the students through problem B, giving less help. Problem B does not have the heavy student prompts that appear in problem A (dotted numbers for the carried digit and the answer).

Does the format specify that any steps are to be repeated? No.

Where are individual turns specified? Individual turns are not specified for this format. The students' written performance should provide a sufficient check of individual mastery.

What kinds of mistakes are the students likely to make, and what correction procedures should be used? The students might give the wrong answer in the first steps or in the New Problem set steps c, f, or g. Use the model-test correction.

The students might have difficulty reading the problem in the second step a, 25 times 3. Use a model-lead-test correction.

The students might say "5" in the second step c. Use a process correction with a previously taught place-value procedure.

- Listen. 15.
- Which digit is in the tens column? (Signal.) *1.*
- That's the digit you carry to the tens column.
- Which digit do you carry to the tens column? (Signal.) *1.*

Format 8:
Division, Lesson 25, EXERCISE 4

Prior to Lesson 25, the students practiced division facts with and without remainders. A division fact with a remainder is the closest fact.

The fact for $5\overline{)11}$ is "5 goes into 11 two times with a remainder."
The students have already learned all the component parts of the 1-digit divisor process.

1. Underline the digit or digits to divide into. In the case of $5\overline{)6627}$, students underline 6 because "the first digit is at least as big as 5." In the case of $5\overline{)4627}$, the students underline 46 because "the first digit is not as big as 5."

2. Write the answer to the closest fact above the last digit that is underlined.

3. Multiply and subtract to find the first remainder.

4. Bring down the next digit (the digit to the right of the underlined digit or digits), and write it to the right of the first remainder.

5. Divide into the new remainder.

6. Write the answer to the right of the first number in the quotient.

7. Multiply and subtract.

8. Recognize that the problem is done when there is an answer above the last digit in the dividend.

The students have also learned to recognize when numbers in the quotient are too large ("the answer is wrong when you can't subtract") or too small ("the remainder must be less than the number in front of the division sign").

> ▶ **EXERCISE 4**
>
> **Operations:** **Working Entire Problems**
>
> a. Find Part 2 on your worksheet.
> b. Find problem A. You're going to work the problem. The problem is done when you have an answer above the last digit in 82. What is the last digit in 82? (Signal.) *2.*

c. Read the problem you're going to work. (Signal.) *5 goes into 82.*
- Underline the first part of that problem. ✔
d. Everybody, what did you underline? (Signal.) *8.*
- Say the underlined problem. (Signal.) *5 goes into 8.*
e. Write the answer above the last underlined digit. ✔
- Everybody, what did you write? (Signal.) *1.*
- Now write the number you're going to subtract from 8 and find the remainder. ✔

$$\begin{array}{r} 1 \\ 5\overline{)82} \\ -5 \\ \hline 3 \end{array}$$

f. Everybody, what's the remainder for the underlined part? (Signal.) *3.*
g. The problem is not done. How do you know? Because you don't have an answer over the last digit of 82. We've worked the underlined part and found a remainder for that part.
- What's the next thing you do after you find a remainder? (Signal.) *Bring down the 2.*
- Do it. ✔
h. Read the new remainder. (Signal.) *32.*
- Say the new problem. (Signal.) *5 goes into 32.*
- Write the answer above the digit you brought down. ✔

$$\begin{array}{r} 16 \\ 5\overline{)82} \\ -5 \\ \hline 32 \end{array}$$

i. Everybody, what did you write above the last digit of 82? (Signal.) *6.*
- Write the number you're going to subtract from 32 and find the remainder. ✔

$$\begin{array}{r} 16 \\ 5\overline{)82} \\ -5 \\ \hline 32 \\ -30 \\ \hline 2 \end{array}$$

j. Everybody, what's the remainder? (Signal.) *2.*
- Have you worked the whole problem? (Signal.) *Yes.*
- (Call on a student.) How do you know? *Because there's a number above the 2.*
k. How many times does 5 go into 82? (Signal.) *16 with a remainder of 2.*

Workbook

A

$$5\overline{)8\,2}$$

What is this format teaching? This format combines all the previously discussed preskills and teaches the entire process of dividing by a 1-digit divisor.

How is it structured? You remind the students how to recognize when a problem is done and then guide them through the steps in solving the problem.

Does the format specify that any steps are to be repeated? No.

Where are individual turns specified? An individual turn is specified in step j.

What kinds of mistakes are the students likely to make, and what correction procedures should be used? The students might write a quotient that is too large, perhaps writing 2 in step e. Use a process correction.

- What's 2 times 5? (Signal.) *10.*
- Are you going to be able to subtract 10 from 8? (Signal.) *No.*
- Remember, your answer is wrong if you can't subtract. Figure out how many times 5 goes into 8 **with** a remainder. (Signal.) *1.*

The students might respond incorrectly in step g. Use a model-test correction.

If the students multiply incorrectly in step i, perhaps writing 25 instead of 30, use a model-test correction.

The students might have difficulty producing the response in step k. Use a model-lead-test correction.

Story Problems

Format 9:
Addition, Lesson 20, EXERCISE 5

Prior to Lesson 20, the students worked picture problems with distracters, such as the following.

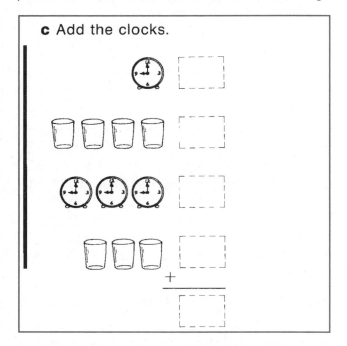

Students have learned to count the objects of the specified class in each row, write the number in the box, cross out each irrelevant row, write a zero in the box, and then add the boxed numbers.

At Lesson 20, begin to work story problems in sentence format.

EXERCISE 5

Story Problems:
Distracters in Word Problems

a. Find Part 5 on your worksheet.
b. These are word problems. You work them just like the picture problems. Look at problem A. Read the directions. (Signal.) *Add the number of shirts Sam sews.*
c. What are you going to add? (Signal.) *The number of shirts Sam sews.*

---

d. Read sentence 1. (Signal.) *Sam sews 5 shirts.*
• Is that about Sam sewing shirts? (Signal.) *Yes.*
e. Read sentence 2. (Signal.) *Sam sells 7 shirts.*
• Is that about Sam sewing shirts? (Signal.) *No.*
• Draw a line through the sentence. ✔
f. Read sentence 3. (Signal.) *Sam buys 3 jackets.*
• Is that about Sam sewing shirts? (Signal.) *No.*
• Draw a line through the sentence. ✔
g. Read sentence 4. (Signal.) *Sam sews 4 shirts.*
• Is that about Sam sewing shirts? (Signal.) *Yes.*
h. Read sentence 5. (Signal.) *Sam sews 1 shirt.*
• Is that about Sam sewing shirts? (Signal.) *Yes.*
i. The sentences that aren't crossed out tell about the number of shirts Sam sews. Write the numbers you're going to add on the lines and write the answer in the box. Remember to write a 0 for each sentence you crossed out. (Pause.) Now work the problem.
• (Check and correct.)
j. How many shirts does Sam sew? (Signal.) *10.*

Workbook

> **A**
>
> Add the number of shirts Sam sews.
>
> 1. Sam sews 5 shirts.   _ _ _ _ _
> 2. Sam sells 7 shirts.   _ _ _ _ _
> 3. Sam buys 3 jackets.   _ _ _ _ _
> 4. Sam sews 4 shirts.   _ _ _ _ _
> 5. Sam sews 1 shirt.   + _ _ _ _ _
>
>   shirts

What is the format teaching? This format is teaching the students to discriminate between sentences in a story problem that are relevant to finding the solution and sentences that are irrelevant.

How is it structured? The students read the directions, and you quiz the students about them. The students then read each sentence in the problem and decide whether it is relevant. If a sentence is not relevant, the teacher instructs them to cross it out. Finally, the students write a number for each relevant sentence, write a zero for each irrelevant sentence, and add the numbers to solve the problem.

Does the format specify that any steps are to be repeated? No.

Where are individual turns specified? Individual turns are not specified for this format. The students' written performance should provide a sufficient check of individual mastery.

What kinds of mistakes are the students likely to make, and what correction procedures should be used? The students might misread the directions in step b (problem A) or the sentences in steps d through h (sentences 1 through 5). Use the model-lead-test correction.

The students might give the wrong answer in step j. If the numbers in the problem were written incorrectly, the students should erase their work, and you should take them through steps b through i again. This constitutes a process correction. If the numbers were written correctly and an addition error was made, use a process correction involving a previously taught procedure for adding columns of single-digit numbers.

- Read the first two numbers you add. (Signal.) *5 and 4.*
- What's 5 plus 4? (Signal.) *9.*
- What number do you add to 9? (Signal.) *1.*
- What's 9 plus 1? (Signal.) *10.*
- So how many shirts did Sam sew? (Signal.) *10.*
- Write that number in the box.

Format 10:
Subtraction, Lesson 37, EXERCISE 8

Prior to Lesson 37, the students learned that given a number family with a missing number, they must write an addition fact if the big number is not given and a subtraction fact if the big number is given.

They also learned that "In subtraction story problems, you start with a big number, and then you make the number smaller. . . . If the number gets smaller, it's a subtraction problem."

The students have used number-family diagrams to help them solve simple action story problems, such as "There are 12 girls playing tennis. 4 go home. How many girls are left?" The students have also practiced an important preskill for classification story problems— identifying the number associated with the class name for "the big number."

EXERCISE 8

Story Problems: Solving Classification Problems Using Number Families

a. Find Part 6 on your worksheet.
b. This story problem has words that are underlined. The words tell you about the number family. I'll read story problem A. Yasmin and her brother own 3 dogs and 4 cats. They have trained them to do tricks. How many pets have they trained?
c. The underlined parts are 3 dogs, 4 cats, how many pets. Which is the name for the big number? (Signal.) *Pets.*
d. Write the names on the lines where they belong. Then write the numbers where they belong. ✔
e. The problem doesn't give the number of pets. That's the big number. If the problem doesn't give the big number, what kind of problem is it? (Signal.) *Addition.*
f. Write the addition problem on the line and figure the answer. Then write the answer in the box. ✔
g. Everybody, read the problem and say the answer. (Signal.) *3 plus 4 equals 7.*

New Problem

a. I'll read story problem B.
Rick was building a tree house for his brother and sister. Rick has 9 tools. He has 4 hammers. The rest are saws. How many saws does he have?

b. The underlined parts are 9 tools, 4 hammers, how many saws. Which is the name for the big number? (Signal.) *Tools.*

c. Write the names on the lines where they belong. Then write the numbers where they belong. ✔

d. Is the big number given? (Signal.) *Yes.*

• So what kind of problem is it? (Signal.) *Subtraction.*

e. Write the subtraction problem on the line and figure the answer. Then write the answer in the box. ✔

f. Everybody, read the problem and say the answer. (Signal.) *9 minus 4 equals 5.*

Workbook

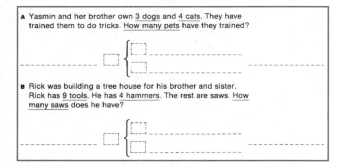

A Yasmin and her brother own 3 dogs and 4 cats. They have trained them to do tricks. How many pets have they trained?

B Rick was building a tree house for his brother and sister. Rick has 9 tools. He has 4 hammers. The rest are saws. How many saws does he have?

What is this format teaching? This format combines all the previously discussed preskills and teaches the entire procedure for using number-family diagrams to solve classification story problems.

How is it structured? You help students translate a story problem into a number-family diagram and determine which operation is called for. The students use the diagram to help them write the problem, and then they solve the problem. The same procedure is repeated for a subtraction story problem.

Does the format specify that any steps are to be repeated? No.

Where are individual turns specified? Individual turns are not specified for this format. The students' written performance should provide a sufficient check of individual mastery.

What kinds of mistakes are the students likely to make, and what correction procedures should be used? The students might give the wrong response in the first step c or the second step b. Use a process correction involving a previously taught classification preskill.

• Listen. Dogs, cats, pets. Dogs are pets, and cats are pets.

• So what is the name for the big number? (Signal.) *Pets.*

If the students give the wrong answer in the first step e, use a model-test correction.

The students might write the problem properly but come up with the wrong answer in the first step f or second step e. Use a model-test correction.

The students might have difficulty saying the problem and answer in step g or the second step f. Use a model-lead-test correction.

Format 11:
Multiplication, Lesson 23, EXERCISE 6

Prior to Lesson 23, the students learned "If you use the same number again and again, you multiply." This rule is first applied to groups of boxes. Later, the students apply the rule to sentences and learn to discriminate between sentences that might be part of a multiplication problem and sentences that might be part of an addition problem.

EXERCISE 6

Story Problems: Working Addition and Multiplication Problems

a. Find Part 6 on your worksheet.

b. Some of these problems are addition problems and some of them are multiplication problems. Let's do the first two problems together.

c. I'll read problem A. There are 9 alarm clocks, 9 wall clocks, and 9 grandfather clocks in that shop. How many clocks are there in all?

d. Is that a multiplication problem? (Signal.) *Yes.*

 • Right. The same number is used again and again.

e. Say the multiplication problem. (Signal.) *9 times 3.*

f. Write the problem and figure the answer. ✔

g. What's the answer? (Signal.) *27.*

 • Write 27 in the box. ✔

h. Read the story problem and find the word that 27 tells about. (Pause.)

i. What word does 27 tell about? (Signal.) *Clocks.*

 • Write it on the line. ✔

j. Read the answer to problem A. (Signal.) *27 clocks.*

New Problem

a. Problem B. There are 5 green flowers, 4 red flowers, and 2 blue flowers in bloom. How many flowers are there in all?

b. Is that a multiplication problem? (Signal.) *No.*

 • Right. The same number is not used again and again. So what kind of problem is it? (Signal.) *Addition.*

c. Say the addition problem. (Signal.) *5 plus 4 plus 2.*

d. Write the problem and figure the answer. ✔

e. What's the answer? (Signal.) *11.*

 • Write 11 in the box. ✔

f. Read the story problem and find the word that 11 tells about. (Pause.)

g. What word does 11 tell about? (Signal.) *Flowers.*

h. Write it on the line. ✔

i. Read the answer to problem B. (Signal.) *11 flowers.*

Workbook

A There are 9 alarm clocks, 9 wall clocks, and 9 grandfather clocks in that shop. How many clocks are there in all?

⌐ ⌐ _ _ _ _ _ _ _ _ _ _ _ _ _ _ _ _ _ _

B There are 5 green flowers, 4 red flowers, and 2 blue flowers in bloom. How many flowers are there in all?

⌐ ⌐ _ _ _ _ _ _ _ _ _ _ _ _ _ _ _ _ _

What is this format teaching? This format combines all previously discussed preskills and teaches the entire procedure for discriminating between multiplication story problems and addition story problems.

How is it structured? You read problem A and guide the students through determining that it is a multiplication problem. The students write the problem and solve it. You then guide them through determining what word in the problem should be written as part of the answer. The same procedure is repeated for problem B, an addition problem.

Does the format specify that any steps are to be repeated? No.

Where are individual turns specified? Individual turns are not specified for this format. The students' written performance should provide a sufficient check of individual mastery.

What kinds of mistakes are the students likely to make, and what correction procedures should be used? The students might give the wrong answer in the first step d or for the first response in the second step b. Use a process correction.

 • Is the same number used again and again? (Signal.) *Yes.*

 • So is it a multiplication problem? (Signal.) *Yes.*

The students might write the wrong answer in the first step f. Use the model-test correction in conjunction with the appropriate fact.

The students might give the wrong answer in the first step i. Use a process correction.

- Listen. 9 alarm **clocks,** 9 wall clocks, and 9 grandfather **clocks.** How many **clocks** are there in all? (Signal.) *27.*
- What word does the answer tell about? (Signal.) *Clocks.*

Format 12:
Division, Lesson 52, EXERCISE 6

Prior to Lesson 52, the students learned to discriminate between multiplication and division problems. "If the big number is given, the problem is a division problem. If the big number is not given, the problem is a multiplication problem." The students have learned that the word that goes with "each" and "every" does not tell about the big number. They have also learned that the number that goes with two different names (such as balls in a bag or books on a shelf) cannot be the big number.

EXERCISE 6

Story Problem Integration: Determining the Correct Sign, Then Working the Problem

a. Find Part 5 on your worksheet. ✔
b. You're going to circle the right sign, write the problem, and figure out the answer.
c. I'll read story A. See whether the story deals with the same number again and again.
- There are 6 kids on each team. There are 48 kids. How many teams are there?
d. Does the story deal with the same number again and again? (Signal.) *Yes.*
- So what two kinds of problems could it be? (Signal.) *Multiplication or division.*
- Underline the right signs. ✔
e. Listen to the story again. See whether the story gives the big number.
- There are 6 kids on each team. There are 48 kids. How many teams are there?

---

f. Does the story give the big number? (Signal.) *Yes.*
- So what kind of problem is it? (Signal.) *Division.*
- Circle the right sign. ✔

New Problem

a. I'll read story B. See whether the story deals with the same number again and again.
- Sherry has some leaves. 8 of them are red and 9 of them are yellow. How many leaves does Sherry have?
b. Does the story deal with the same number again and again? (Signal.) *No.*
- So what two kinds of problems could it be? (Signal.) *Addition or subtraction.*
- Underline the right signs. ✔
c. Listen to the story again. See whether the story gives the big number.
- Sherry has some leaves. 8 of them are red and 9 of them are yellow. How many leaves does Sherry have?
d. Does the story give the big number? (Signal.) *No.*
- So what kind of problem is it? (Signal.) *Addition.*
- Circle the right sign. ✔

Workbook

A There are 6 kids on each team. There are 48 kids. How many teams are there?
$+ \quad - \quad \times \quad \div$

B Sherry has some leaves. 8 of them are red and 9 of them are yellow. How many leaves does Sherry have?
$+ \quad - \quad \times \quad \div$

What is this format teaching? This format is teaching the application of the procedure for determining the operation called for in a story problem.

1. Is the same number used again and again?
No = addition or subtraction.
Yes = multiplication or division.

2. Is the big number given?
No = addition or multiplication.
Yes = subtraction or division.

How is it structured? You read the first problem and guide the students through making the discriminations. Because the same number is used again and again, the students underline the multiplication and division signs. Then they circle the division sign because the big number is given. The procedure is repeated with the second problem, an addition problem. The students underline the addition and subtraction signs because the same number is not used again and again. Then they circle the addition sign because the big number is not given.

Does the format specify that any steps are to be repeated? No.

Where are individual turns specified? Individual turns are not specified for this format. The students' written performance should provide a sufficient check of individual mastery.

What kinds of mistakes are the students likely to make, and what correction procedures should be used? The students might say "No" as the first response in the first step d. Use a process correction.

- Remember, the word **each** tells you that the same number is used again and again. Listen. There are 6 kids on **each** team. There are 48 kids. How many teams are there? Does the story use the word **each**? (Signal.) *Yes.*
- So does the story deal with the same number again and again? (Signal.) *Yes.*

The students might say "Subtraction" for the second response in the second step d. Use a process correction.

- Remember, if the story doesn't give the big number, it's an addition problem. This story doesn't give the big number, so what kind of problem is it? (Signal.) *Addition.*

Naming Problems

Format 13:
Basic Fractions, Lesson 6,
EXERCISE 1

EXERCISE 1

Fraction Naming

a. (Write on the board:)

$$\frac{5}{4}$$

- (Touch the 5.) This fraction is 5 (touch the 4) fourths.
- Read this fraction. *5 fourths.*

b. (Change the 5 to a 3.)
- (Touch the 3.) This fraction is 3 (touch the 4) fourths.
- Read this fraction. *3 fourths.*

c. (Change the 3 to a 6.)
- Read this fraction. *6 fourths.*

d. (Write on the board:)

$$\frac{3}{7}$$

- This fraction is 3 sevenths.
- How do you read this fraction? (Signal.) *3 sevenths.*

e. (Change the 3 to an 8.)
- How do you read this fraction? (Signal.) *8 sevenths.*

f. (Write on the board:)

$$\frac{1}{6}$$

- This fraction is 1 sixth.
- How do you read this fraction? (Signal.) *1 sixth.*

g. (Change the 1 to a 7.)
- How do you read this fraction? (Signal.) *7 sixths.*

h. (Write on the board:)
★
$$\frac{6}{4} \quad \frac{3}{6} \quad \frac{5}{7} \quad \frac{9}{7} \quad \frac{2}{4} \quad \frac{7}{6}$$

- Read each fraction when I touch it. (Touch each fraction.)
- (Repeat any that are difficult.)

What is this format teaching? This format is teaching the students to name fractions.

How is it structured? This format is taught with students looking up at the board. You have written examples of fractions on the board and will use a "point/touch" signal to elicit responses from the students. Begin the exercise by modeling the procedure of naming fractions by pointing to each part and telling students what each part is named. After several examples, lead the students in naming additional fractions. Students then practice the skill by naming a list of fractions on your point/touch cue.

Does the format specify that any steps are to be repeated? Yes, the last step specifies to repeat any fractions that are difficult for the students to name without error.

Where are individual turns specified? Individual turns are not specified for this format.

What kinds of mistakes are the students likely to make, and what correction procedures should be used? The students might give the incorrect response at step g. Use the model-test correction.

- Listen. 7 sixths.
- How do you read this fraction? (Signal.) *7 sixths.*

Sample Lessons

Lesson 30

EXERCISE 1

Facts: Independent Practice

a. Open your workbook to Lesson 30. Find Part 1.
b. Touch the first problem. Read the problem and say the answer. (Signal.) *7 plus 3 equals 10.*
c. Touch the next problem. Read the problem and say the answer. (Signal.) *7 plus 1 equals 8.*
d. Touch the next problem. Read the problem and say the answer. (Signal.) *7 plus 5 equals 12.*
e. Touch the next problem. Read the problem and say the answer. (Signal.) *7 plus 4 equals 11.*
f. Touch the next problem. Read the problem and say the answer. (Signal.) *7 plus 2 equals 9.*
g. (Repeat steps b–f until firm.)
h. Write the answers to all of the problems in Part 1. You have one minute. Get ready. Go.
i. (After one minute, say:) Stop. Raise your hand if you worked all the problems. If you didn't finish, put an **X** next to each problem you didn't get to. (Pause.) Now work the rest of the problems.
j. Let's check your work. Read each problem and say the answer. Put an **X** next to each problem you got wrong.
k. First problem. (Signal.) *7 plus 3 equals 10.*
l. Next problem. (Signal.) *7 plus 1 equals 8.*
m. (Repeat step l for the rest of the problems in Part 1. See *Answer Key*.)
n. Raise your hand if you answered all the problems in one minute and didn't get any wrong. (Praise students.)

EXERCISE 2

Facts: Number Families in a Series

a. Find Part 2 on your worksheet.
b. In all these number families, the big number is not given. For each number family, say the fact that starts with 5.
c. Look at family A. Say the fact. (Signal.) *5 plus 9 equals 14.*
d. Family B. Say the fact. (Signal.) *5 plus 6 equals 11.*
e. Family C. Say the fact. (Signal.) *5 plus 8 equals 13.*
f. Family D. Say the fact. (Signal.) *5 plus 7 equals 12.*
g. (Repeat steps c–f until firm.)
h. Write the big number for each of the number families in Part 2. Then write both the facts.
• (Check and correct. See *Answer Key*.)
i. Let's check your work. Put an **X** next to each fact you got wrong.
j. Family A. Read the fact that starts with 5. (Signal.) *5 plus 9 equals 14.*
• Read the fact that starts with 9. (Signal.) *9 plus 5 equals 14.*
k. (Repeat step j for the rest of the number families in Part 2. See *Answer Key*.)

EXERCISE 3

Facts: Figuring Out Complex Facts

a. Find Part 3 on your worksheet.
b. Read problem A. (Signal.) *15 plus 3.*
• Read the ones column and say the answer. (Signal.) *5 plus 3 equals 8.*
• Read problem A and say the answer. (Signal.) *15 plus 3 equals 18.*
c. Read problem B. (Signal.) *12 plus 5.*
• Read the ones column and say the answer. (Signal.) *2 plus 5 equals 7.*
• Read problem B and say the answer. (Signal.) *12 plus 5 equals 17.*
d. Read problem C. (Signal.) *41 plus 7.*
• Read the ones column and say the answer. (Signal.) *1 plus 7 equals 8.*
• Read problem C and say the answer. (Signal.) *41 plus 7 equals 48.*
e. Read problem D. (Signal.) *11 plus 3.*
• Read the ones column and say the answer. (Signal.) *1 plus 3 equals 4.*
• Read problem D and say the answer. (Signal.) *11 plus 3 equals 14.*

f. Read problem E. (Signal.) *74 plus 5.*
● Read the ones column and say the answer. (Signal.) *4 plus 5 equals 9.*
● Read problem E and say the answer. (Signal.) *74 plus 5 equals 79.*

g. Let's see if you can figure out the answers without looking at the problems. Close your workbook. Listen. 15 plus 3. What does 15 plus 3 equal? (Signal.) *18.*
● 12 plus 5. What does 12 plus 5 equal? (Signal.) *17.*
● 41 plus 7. What does 41 plus 7 equal? (Signal.) *48.*
● 11 plus 3. What does 11 plus 3 equal? (Signal.) *14.*
● 74 plus 5. What does 74 plus 5 equal? (Signal.) *79.*

h. Open your workbook again to Lesson 30. Find Part 3.

i. Write the answers to all of the problems in Part 3.
● (Check and correct. See *Answer Key.*)

j. (Review answers orally with the entire group. See *Answer Key.*)

EXERCISE 4

Timing Format

a. Find Part 4 on your worksheet.

b. You're going to say the answers to some facts. Touch the first problem and get ready to tell me the answer. (Pause.) What's the answer? (Signal.) *11.*

c. Next problem. (Pause.) What's the answer? (Signal.) *13.*

d. (Repeat step c until firm for the rest of the problems in the first row. See *Answer Key.*)

e. Let's see how fast you can work these problems. You have one minute. Get ready. Go.

f. (After one minute, say:) Stop. Put an **X** next to each problem you didn't get to.

g. Let's check your work. You're going to read each problem and say the answer. If you have the wrong answer, put an **X** next to the problem.

h. First problem. (Signal.) *5 plus 6 equals 11.*

i. Next problem. (Signal.) *5 plus 8 equals 13.*

j. (Repeat step i for the rest of the problems in Part 4. See *Answer Key.*)

EXERCISE 5

Place Value: Determining Number of Tens—Verbal

a. I'll say some numbers. You tell me how many tens are in each number. You have to think about how each number is written.

b. 21. How many tens are in 21? (Signal.) *2.*

   To Correct
   Think how you write 21. How many tens are in the tens column? (Signal.) *2.*◀

c. 18. How many tens are in 18? (Signal.) *1.*

d. 14. How many tens are in 14? (Signal.) *1.*

e. 36. How many tens are in 36? (Signal.) *3.*

f. 24. How many tens are in 24? (Signal.) *2.*

g. 17. How many tens are in 17? (Signal.) *1.*

h. 13. How many tens are in 13? (Signal.) *1.*

i. (Repeat steps b–h until firm.)

j. (Call on individual students. Each student is to tell the number of tens in randomly selected numbers.)

EXERCISE 6

Place Value: Reading Hundreds and Thousands Numbers

a. Find Part 5 on your worksheet.

b. How many digits are in item A? (Signal.) *4.*
● Read that number. (Signal.) *Four thousand.*

c. How many digits are in item B? (Signal.) *3.*
● Read that number. (Signal.) *Four hundred.*

d. How many digits are in item C? (Signal.) *3.*
● Read that number. (Signal.) *Three hundred eighteen.*

e. How many digits are in item D? (Signal.) *4.*
● Read that number. (Signal.) *One thousand one hundred fifty.*

f. How many digits are in item E? (Signal.) *4.*
● Read that number. (Signal.) *Two thousand three hundred fourteen.*

g. Read item F. (Signal.) *One hundred seven.*
h. Read item G. (Signal.) *Two thousand three hundred sixty.*
i. (Call on individual students. Each student is to read all the numbers in Part 5.)

EXERCISE 7

Operations: Renaming the Ones Column and Working the Problem

a. Find Part 6 on your worksheet.
b. You have to carry to work the problems in Part 6. I'll work two problems with you.
c. Look at problem A. When you add numbers in columns, which column do you start with? (Signal.) *The ones column.*
d. Add the ones column and get ready to tell me the answer. (Pause.) What's the answer for the ones column? (Signal.) *15.*
e. What do you write in the ones column? (Signal.) *5.*
f. What do you carry to the tens column? (Signal.) *1 ten.*
g. Do it and finish working the problem. ✔
h. What's the answer to problem A? (Signal.) *105.*

New Problem

a. Look at problem B. When you add numbers in columns, which column do you start with? (Signal.) *The ones column.*
b. Add the ones column and get ready to tell me the answer. (Pause.)
• What's the answer for the ones column? (Signal.) *20.*
c. What do you write in the ones column? (Signal.) *0.*
• What do you carry to the tens column? (Signal.) *2 tens.*
d. Do it and finish working the problem. ✔
e. What's the answer to problem B? (Signal.) *100.*
f. Work the rest of the problems in Part 6 on your own.
• (Check and correct. See *Answer Key.*)
g. Let's check your work. I'll read the answers. Put an **X** next to each problem you got wrong.

h. Problem C. The answer is 124.
• Problem D. The answer is 120.

EXERCISE 8

Story Problems: Practicing the Addition-Subtraction Discrimination

a. Find Part 7 on your worksheet. These problems are tricky. Some of the sentences don't tell about adding. They tell about subtracting or taking away things.
b. Look at problem A. Find the directions. (Pause.) Read the directions. (Signal.) *Add the things that Sharon got.*
• You have to think about the different ways you can get things.
c. Read sentence 1. (Signal.) *Sharon lost 4 pencils.*
• Is that about Sharon getting things? (Signal.) *No.*
• Draw a line through it. ✔
d. Read sentence 2. (Signal.) *Sharon gave away 9 pencils.*
• Is that about Sharon getting things? (Signal.) *No.*
• Draw a line through it. ✔
e. Read sentence 3. (Signal.) *Sharon found 2 pieces of paper.*
• Is that about Sharon getting things? (Signal.) *Yes.*
f. Read sentence 4. (Signal.) *Sharon threw away 5 crayons.*
• Is that about Sharon getting things? (Signal.) *No.*
• Draw a line through it. ✔
g. Read sentence 5. (Signal.) *Sharon bought 8 pens.*
• Is that about Sharon getting things? (Signal.) *Yes.*
h. Write the numbers you are going to add. Then work the problem. Don't forget to write the word that's part of the answer.
i. Read the answer. (Signal.) *10 things.*
j. Work the rest of the problems in Part 7 on your own.
• (Check and correct. See *Answer Key.*)

k. Let's check your work. I'll read the answers. Put an **X** next to each problem you got wrong.
l. Problem B. The answer is 19 things.
- Problem C. The answer is 54 games.
- Problem D. The answer is 117 times.

EXERCISE 9

Preparation for Mastery Test: Facts

a. When we do the next lesson, you're going to have a test on addition facts. Let's go over some facts together.
b. I'll say the problems and you give the answers. What does 4 plus 10 equal? Get ready. (Signal.) *14.*
c. (Repeat step b for the following problems:)

$$\begin{array}{cccccc} 2 & 1 & 5 & 8 & 3 & 9 \\ +10 & +10 & +10 & +10 & +10 & +10 \end{array}$$

$$\begin{array}{cccccc} 6 & 7 & 5 & 5 & 5 & 5 \\ +10 & +10 & +7 & +9 & +8 & +6 \end{array}$$

d. Remember those facts for the test.

EXERCISE 10

Workcheck

a. Now we're going to figure out the number of points you earned for this lesson.
b. Count the number of facts you got wrong in Parts 1, 2, and 4.
c. Find the beginning of your worksheet for Lesson 30.
d. If you got 0 or 1 wrong, you get 3 points. If you got 2 wrong, you get 1 point. If you got more than 2 wrong, you get 0 points.
e. Write the number of points you earned in the box labeled "Facts."
f. Now count the number of problems you got wrong in Parts 6 and 7.
g. Once again find the beginning of your worksheet for Lesson 30. You are going to write the number of points you earned in the box labeled "Problems."

h. If you got 0 wrong, you get 5 points. If you got 1 wrong, you get 3 points. If you got more than 1 wrong, you get 0 points.
i. Write the number of points you earned in the box labeled "Problems."
j. (If Fact Game bonus points are to be added to the "Bonus" box in this lesson, do not do steps k and l.)
k. Add up all of the points in the boxes and put the answer in the box labeled "Total." This is the number of points you earned for this lesson.
l. Turn to the Point Summary Charts on the inside back cover of your workbook. Find the empty box below Lesson 30. Write the total number of points you earned in that box.
m. (Have the students total their points for Lessons 26–30.)

EXERCISE 11

Fact Game

a. (When you're ready to begin playing, divide the class into groups. Depending on the size of your class, there will be four or fewer students in each group plus a student who will be judge. For each group you will need: one die or spinner numbered from 1 through 6, a score sheet, and a pencil. Write the answers to the facts shown in step b on a blank sheet of paper. This paper will also serve as the group's score sheet.)
b. (Write the following problems on the board:)

$$\begin{array}{cccccc} \textbf{1. } 5 & \textbf{2. } 5 & \textbf{3. } 5 & \textbf{4. } 5 & \textbf{5. } 5 & \textbf{6. } 5 \\ +5 & +6 & +7 & +8 & +9 & +10 \end{array}$$

c. (Give each team a die or spinner and give each judge a pencil and a sheet of paper with the answers.)
d. We're going to play a game called the Fact Game. You can earn up to 2 bonus points each day we play.
e. These are the rules of the game. All of the teams play the game at the same time. Each team starts by having one player roll the die or spin the spinner. The number that

the die or spin the spinner. The number that comes up tells which problem on the board that player must give the answer for. For example, if a 4 comes up on the spinner or die, you read problem 4, 5 plus 8, and then give the answer. What do you do if a 2 comes up? (Signal.) *Read problem 2 and give the answer.*

f. If the answer is correct, the judge draws one line on the sheet of paper.

g. If the answer is incorrect, the judge crosses out two lines. (Be aware that when the first turn is taken there will be no lines to cross out.)

h. How many lines does a judge draw for the correct answer? (Signal.) *One.*

• How many lines does a judge cross out for the wrong answer? (Signal.) *Two.*

i. Take turns answering the problems until I say "Stop." You will play for five minutes.

j. After I say "Stop," the judge will count up the team's lines.

k. (Pick a team and model the game for the rest of the students.) I'll play the game with this team. Everybody else should watch how we play.

l. (After you finish demonstrating the game, say:) When I signal, start playing. I'll tell you to stop at the end of five minutes. If you have any questions, raise your hand. (Signal.)

m. (Check each group during the game.)

n. (After five minutes are up, say:) Stop playing.

o. Judges, count the number of lines the team got and write the total at the top of the sheet of paper.

p. If your team got 30, 31, 32, 33, 34, 35, 36, 37, 38, or 39 lines, you get 1 point. If your team has 40 or more lines, you get 2 points. All judges get 2 points.

q. Write your points in the "Bonus" box at the beginning of your lesson for today. (Be aware that you might have already awarded some bonus points earlier in the lesson either for appropriate group behavior or for very good worksheet performance.)

r. Add up all of the points in the boxes and put the answer in the box labeled "Total." This is the number of points you earned for this lesson.

s. Turn to the inside back cover of your workbook. ✔
Find the empty box below Lesson 30. Write the total number of points you earned in that box. ✔

t. (Have the students total their points for Lessons 26–30.)

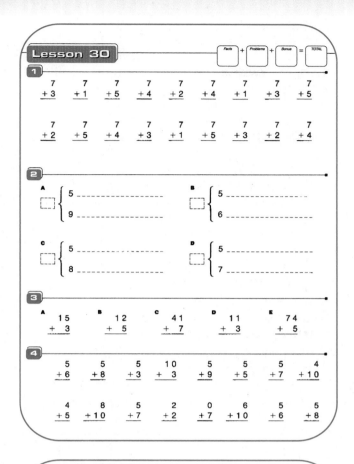

Facts + Problems + Bonus = TOTAL

1

7	7	7	7	7	7	7	7	7
+3	+1	+5	+4	+2	+4	+1	+3	+5

7	7	7	7	7	7	7	7	7
+2	+5	+4	+3	+1	+5	+3	+2	+4

2

A { 5 ------------------
   { 9 ------------------

B { 5 ------------------
   { 6 ------------------

C { 5 ------------------
   { 8 ------------------

D { 5 ------------------
   { 7 ------------------

3

A 15	B 12	C 41	D 11	E 74
+ 3	+ 5	+ 7	+ 3	+ 5

4

5	5	5	10	5	5	5	4
+6	+8	+3	+ 3	+9	+5	+7	+10

4	8	5	2	0	6	5	5
+5	+10	+7	+2	+7	+10	+6	+8

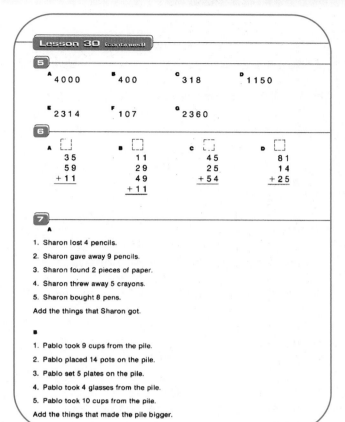

5

A 4000	B 400	C 318	D 1150

E 2314	F 107	G 2360

6

A ⬜	B ⬜	C ⬜	D ⬜
35	11	45	81
59	29	25	14
+ 11	49	+ 54	+ 25
	+ 11		

7

A
1. Sharon lost 4 pencils.
2. Sharon gave away 9 pencils.
3. Sharon found 2 pieces of paper.
4. Sharon threw away 5 crayons.
5. Sharon bought 8 pens.
Add the things that Sharon got.

B
1. Pablo took 9 cups from the pile.
2. Pablo placed 14 pots on the pile.
3. Pablo set 5 plates on the pile.
4. Pablo took 4 glasses from the pile.
5. Pablo took 10 cups from the pile.
Add the things that made the pile bigger.

C
1. Team 1 won 13 games in May.
2. Team 2 won 14 games in May.
3. Team 1 won 20 games in June.
4. Team 1 lost 8 games in June.
5. Team 1 won 21 games in July.
Add the games team 1 won.

D
1. The boys carried boxes 52 times.
2. The boys raked leaves 42 times.
3. The boys chopped wood 11 times.
4. The boys played catch 18 times.
5. The girls raked leaves 24 times.
6. The boys piled wood 12 times.
How many times did the boys do work?

EXERCISE 1

Facts: Practicing New Facts

a. Open your workbook to Lesson 30. Find Part 1.

b. Touch the first problem. Read the problem and say the answer. (Signal.) *12 minus 9 equals 3.*

c. Touch the next problem. Read the problem and say the answer. (Signal.) *17 minus 9 equals 8.*

d. (Repeat step c until firm for the rest of the problems in the first row. See *Answer Key.*)

e. This time just tell me the answers.

f. First problem. What's the answer? (Signal.) *3.*

g. Next problem. What's the answer? (Signal.) *8.*

h. (Repeat step g until firm for the rest of the problems. See *Answer Key.*)

i. Now write the answers to the problems in Part 1. Get ready. Go.

• (Check and correct. See *Answer Key.*)

j. Let's check your work. Read each problem and say the answer. Put an **X** next to each problem you got wrong.

k. First problem. (Signal.) *12 minus 9 equals 3.*

l. Next problem. (Signal.) *17 minus 9 equals 8.*

m. (Repeat step l for the rest of the problems in Part 3. See *Answer Key.*)

EXERCISE 2

Facts: Filling in Numbers in Number Families

a. Find Part 2 on your worksheet.

b. Each problem gives two numbers of a number family. I'll read problem A. The big number is 7. A small number is 4.

c. What kind of number is 7? (Signal.) *The big number.*

• Write 7 in the box for the big number. ✔

d. What kind of number is 4? (Signal.) *A small number.*

• Write 4 in the top box for small numbers. ✔

e. I'll read problem B. A small number is 10. Another small number is 5.

f. Both numbers are small numbers. Write them in the boxes for the small numbers. ✔

g. Write the numbers for the rest of the number families in Part 2 where they belong. Don't write the problems.

• (Check and correct. See *Answer Key.*)

h. Let's check your work. I'll put the answers on the board. Put an **X** next to each problem you got wrong. (Write the answers on the board. See *Answer Key.*)

EXERCISE 3

Story Problems: Rules for Adding and Subtracting

a. (Continue with worksheet Part 2.) Touch number family A again. ✔

• Is the big number given? (Signal.) *Yes.*

• So what kind of problem are you going to write? (Signal.) *Subtraction.*

b. I'll say the problem without the answer. 7 minus 4 equals how many? Say the problem. (Signal.) *7 minus 4 equals how many?*

c. Write the problem and draw a box for how many. ✔

New Problem

a. Touch number family B. ✔

• Is the big number given? (Signal.) *No.*

• So what kind of problem are you going to write? (Signal.) *Addition.*

b. Say the problem without the answer. (Signal.) *10 plus 5 equals how many?*

• (Repeat step b until firm.)

c. Yes, 10 plus 5 equals how many? Write the problem and draw a box for how many. ✔

New Problem

a. Touch number family C. ✔

• Is the big number given? (Signal.) *No.*

• So what kind of problem are you going to write? (Signal.) *Addition.*

b. Say the problem without the answer. (Signal.) *7 plus 3 equals how many?*

• (Repeat step b until firm.)

c. Write the problem and draw a box for how many. ✔

d. Write the rest of the problems in Part 2 on your own. Then figure the answers.

• (Check and correct. See *Answer Key.*)

e. Let's check your work. Read each problem and say the answer. Put an **X** next to each problem you got wrong.

f. Number family A. Say the number problem you wrote. (Signal.) *7 minus 4 equals 3.*

g. (Repeat step f for the rest of the problems in Part 2. See *Answer Key.*)

EXERCISE 4

Timing Format

a. Find Part 3 on your worksheet.

b. You're going to say the answers to some facts. Touch the first problem and get ready to tell me the answer. (Pause.) What's the answer? (Signal.) *4.*

c. Next problem. (Pause.) What's the answer? (Signal.) *4.*

d. (Repeat step c until firm for the rest of the problems in the first row. See *Answer Key.*)

e. Let's see how fast you can work these problems. You have one minute. Get ready. Go.

f. (After one minute, say:) Stop. Put an **X** next to each problem you didn't get to.

g. Let's check your work. You're going to read each problem and say the answer. If you have the wrong answer, put an **X** next to the problem.

h. First problem. (Signal.) *12 minus 8 equals 4.*

i. Next problem. (Signal.) *7 minus 3 equals 4.*

j. (Repeat step i for the rest of the problems in Part 3. See *Answer Key.*)

EXERCISE 5

Mastery Test: Number Families

a. Today you're going to have a test on writing a problem for each number family.

b. Find Part 4 on your worksheet. Don't start until I signal.

c. You'll have one and a half minutes to complete Part 4.

d. You may start working now. (Signal.)

e. (At the end of one and a half minutes, say:) Stop.

f. Let's check your work. I'll read the answers to the problems in Part 4. Put an **X** next to each problem you got wrong.

g. Problem A. The fact is 4 plus 3 equals 7.

h. (Repeat step g for the rest of the problems in Part 4. See *Answer Key.*)

i. Count the number of facts you got wrong.

j. (Draw the following on the board:)

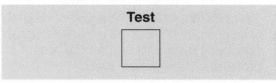

k. Find the beginning of your worksheet for Lesson 30.

l. If you got all of the facts correct, you get 2 points. If you got any facts wrong, you get 0 points.

m. Write the number of points you earned in the box like this. (Point to the box you've drawn on the board. Check to see that the students have recorded their points correctly.)

Remediation Directions

a. (Record the number of errors each student made on the Mastery Test Record Chart.)

b. (If more than 20 percent of the students missed 2 or more items, you should review Lesson 27, Exercise 7 and Lesson 28, Exercise 5. Because students will have already used their worksheets, duplicates appear in the back of the *Workbook*. Ask the students to find the heading "Mastery Test Review—Lesson 30" at the back of their workbooks. Part 1 corresponds to Lesson 27, Exercise 7, and Part 2 to Lesson 28, Exercise 5. Use the new part numbers when presenting the exercises.)

c. (If no more than 20 percent of the students missed 2 or more items, present Lesson 31 during the next class period.)

EXERCISE 6

Facts: Practicing New Facts

a. Find Part 5 on your worksheet.

b. Touch the first problem. Read the problem and say the answer. (Signal.) *16 minus 7 equals 9.*

c. Touch the next problem. Read the problem and say the answer. (Signal.) *8 minus 5 equals 3.*

d. (Repeat step c until firm for the rest of the problems. See *Answer Key.*)

e. This time just tell me the answers.

f. First problem. What's the answer? (Signal.) *9.*

g. Next problem. What's the answer? (Signal.) *3.*

h. (Repeat step g until firm for the rest of the problems. See *Answer Key.*)

i. Now write the answers to the problems in Part 5. Get ready. Go.

• (Check and correct. See *Answer Key.*)

j. Let's check your work. Read each problem and say the answer.

k. First problem. (Signal.) *16 minus 7 equals 9.*

l. Next problem. (Signal.) *8 minus 5 equals 3.*

m. (Repeat step l for the rest of the problems in Part 5. See *Answer Key.*)

EXERCISE 7

Place Value: Reading Thousands Numbers

a. Find Part 6 on your worksheet.

b. These are thousands numbers. Thousands numbers have four digits. I'll read the first thousands number. You'll read the rest of them.

c. Item A is one thousand thirty-five.

d. Everybody, read item B. (Signal.) *Two thousand four hundred six.*

• Read item C. (Signal.) *Three thousand six.*

• Read item D. (Signal.) *Five thousand seventy-one.*

• Read item E. (Signal.) *Three thousand four hundred one.*

• (Repeat step d until firm.)

e. (Call on individual students. Each student is to read all the numbers in Part 6.)

EXERCISE 8

Story Problems: Determining What Kind of Number Is Given—Written Practice

a. Find Part 7 on your worksheet.

b. Problem A.
Ann had 9 oranges. She gave 4 oranges to her friends.

• What kind of problem is it? (Signal.) *Subtraction.*

c. If it's a subtraction problem, is the big number given? (Signal.) *Yes.*

d. I'll read the problem again.
Ann had 9 oranges. She gave 4 oranges to her friends.

• Is 9 the big number or a small number? (Signal.) *The big number.*

• What kind of number is 4? (Signal.) *A small number.*

e. (Repeat steps b–d until firm.)

f. Fill in the blanks for problem A. ✔

New Problem

a. Problem B.
Jack has 7 books. He buys 2 books.

• What kind of problem is it? (Signal.) *Addition.*

b. If it's an addition problem, is the big number given? (Signal.) *No.*

c. I'll read the problem again.
Jack has 7 books. He buys 2 books.

• Is 7 the big number or a small number? (Signal.) *A small number.*

• What kind of number is 2? (Signal.) *A small number.*

d. (Repeat steps a–c until firm.)

e. Fill in the blanks for problem B. ✔

f. Fill in the blanks for the rest of the problems in Part 7 on your own.

• (Check and correct. See *Answer Key.*)

g. Let's check your work. Read the sentences you filled in. Put an **X** next to each problem you got wrong.

h. Problem C. (Signal.) 4 is the big number. *1 is a small number.*

i. (Repeat step h for the rest of the problems in Part 7. See *Answer Key.*)

EXERCISE 9

Operations: Determining When to Borrow from Two Digits

a. Find Part 8 on your worksheet.

b. All the problems in Part 8 have zeroes, but in some of the problems you don't have to borrow from two digits.

c. Look at problem A. (Pause.) Read the problem in the ones column. (Signal.) *2 minus 4.*

• Do you have to borrow? (Signal.) *Yes.*

• What do you borrow from? (Signal.) *80.*

d. Look at problem B. (Pause.) Read the problem in the ones column. (Signal.) *4 minus 3.*

• Do you have to borrow? (Signal.) *No.*

e. Read the problem in the tens column. (Signal.) *0 minus 5.*

• Do you have to borrow? (Signal.) *Yes.*

• What do you borrow from? (Signal.) *7.*

f. (Repeat steps c–e until firm.)

g. Look at problem C. (Pause.) Read the problem in the ones column. (Signal.) *4 minus 1.*

• Do you have to borrow? (Signal.) *No.*

h. Read the problem in the tens column. (Signal.) *8 minus 9.*

• Do you have to borrow? (Signal.) *Yes.*

• What do you borrow from? (Signal.) *60.*

i. (Repeat steps g and h until firm.)

j. Look at problem D. (Pause.) Read the problem in the ones column. (Signal.) *3 minus 3.*

• Do you have to borrow? (Signal.) *No.*

k. Read the problem in the tens column. (Signal.) *6 minus 5.*

• Do you have to borrow? (Signal.) *No.*

l. Read the problem in the hundreds column. (Signal.) *0 minus 1.*

• Do you have to borrow? (Signal.) *Yes.*

• What do you borrow from? (Signal.) *8.*

m. (Repeat steps j–l until firm.)

n. Work the problems in Part 8 on your own.

• (Check and correct. See *Answer Key*.)

o. Let's check your work. Put an **X** next to each problem you got wrong.

p. Problem A. What's the answer? (Signal.) *618.*

q. (Repeat step p for the rest of the problems in Part 6. See *Answer Key*.)

EXERCISE 10

Independent Work

• Do Part 9. (The students can work this part without supervision.)

EXERCISE 11

Workcheck

a. Now we're going to figure out the number of points you've earned for this lesson.

b. Count the number of facts you got wrong in Parts 1, 2, and 3.

c. Find the beginning of your worksheet for Lesson 30.

d. If you got 0 or 1 wrong, you get 3 points. If you got 2 wrong, you get 1 point. If you got more than 2 wrong, you get 0 points.

e. Write the number of points you earned in the box labeled "Facts."

f. Now we'll check all of the problems in Part 9.

g. Put an **X** next to each problem you got wrong.

h. (Read the answers from the *Answer Key* for Lesson 30, Part 9.)

i. Now count the number of problems you got wrong in Parts 7, 8, and 9.

j. Once again find the beginning of your worksheet for Lesson 30. You are going to write the number of points you earned in the box labeled "Problems."

k. If you got 0 or 1 wrong, you get 5 points. If you got 2, 3, or 4 wrong, you get 3 points. If you got more than 4 wrong, you get 0 points.

l. Write the number of points you earned in the box labeled "Problems."

m. (If Fact Game bonus points are to be added to the "Bonus" box in this lesson, do not do steps n–p.)

n. Add up all of the points in the boxes and put the answer in the box labeled "Total." This is the number of points you've earned for this lesson.

o. Turn to the Point Summary Charts on the inside back cover of your workbook. Find the empty box below Lesson 30. Write the total number of points you earned in that box.

p. (Have the students total their points for Lessons 26–30.)

EXERCISE 12

Fact Game

a. (When you're ready to begin playing, divide the class into groups. Depending on the size of your class, there will be four or fewer students in each group plus a student who will be the judge. For each group you will need: one die or spinner numbered from 1 through 6, a score sheet, and a pencil. Write the answers to the facts shown in step b on a blank sheet of paper. This paper will also serve as the group's score sheet.

b. (Write the following problems on the board:)

1. 12	2. 12	3. 12	4. 12	5. 12	6. 12
− 3	− 4	− 5	− 7	− 8	− 9

c. (Give each team a die or spinner and give each judge a pencil and a sheet of paper with the answers.)

d. We're going to play a game called the Fact Game. You can earn up to 2 bonus points each day we play.

e. These are the rules of the game. All of the teams play the game at the same time. Each team starts by having one player roll the die or spin the spinner. The number that comes up tells which problem on the board that player must give the answer for. For example, if a 4 comes up on the spinner or die, you read problem 4, 12 minus 7, and then give the answer. What do you do if a 2 comes up? (Signal.) *Read problem 2 and give the answer.*

f. If the answer is correct, the judge draws 1 line on the sheet of paper.

g. If the answer is incorrect, the judge crosses out 2 lines. **(Be aware that when the first turn is taken there will be no lines to cross out.)**

h. How many lines does a judge draw for the correct answer? (Signal.) *1.*

• How many lines does a judge cross out for the wrong answer? (Signal.) *2.*

i. Take turns answering the problems until I say "Stop." You will play for five minutes.

j. After I say "Stop," the judge will count up the team's lines.

k. (Pick a team and model the game for the rest of the students.) I'll play the game with this team. Everyone else should watch how we play.

l. (After you finish demonstrating the game, say:) When I signal, start playing. I'll tell you to stop at the end of five minutes. If you have any questions, raise your hand. (Signal.)

m. (Check each group during the game.)

n. (After five minutes are up, say:) Stop playing.

o. Judges, count up the number of lines your team got and write the total at the top of your sheet of paper.

p. If your team got 30, 31, 32, 33, 34, 35, 36, 37, 38, or 39 lines, you get 1 point. If your team has 40 or more lines, you get 2 points. All judges get 2 points.

q. Write your points in the "Bonus" box at the beginning of your lesson for today.

r. (You might want to write numbers in the boxes on the board and demonstrate this next step.) Add up all of the points in the boxes and put the answer in the box labeled "Total." This is the number of points you earned for this lesson.

s. Turn to the Point Summary Charts on the inside back cover of your workbook. ✔ Find the empty box below Lesson 27. Write the total number of points you earned in that box. ✔

t. (Have the students total their points for Lessons 26–30)

Lesson 30

| Test | + | Facts | + | Problems | + | Bonus | = | TOTAL |

1

```
 12      17      14      16      11      18      15      13
- 9     - 9     - 9     - 9     - 9     - 9     - 9     - 9

 11      17      13      16      12      15      18      14
- 9     - 9     - 9     - 9     - 9     - 9     - 9     - 9
```

2

A
The big number is 7. A small number is 4.

B
A small number is 10. Another small number is 5.

C
A small number is 7. Another small number is 3.

D
The big number is 10. A small number is 2.

E
The big number is 5. A small number is 4.

F
A small number is 8. Another small number is 2.

Lesson 30 (continued)

3

```
 12       7      12      12      12       7      10      14
- 8      - 3     - 7     - 4     - 5     - 5     - 3     - 6

 12      12      12       7      12      12      12       7
- 3      - 7     - 5     - 6     - 8     - 4     - 5     - 5
```

4

A
{ 4 / 3

B
7 { 2 / □

C
9 { 8 / □

D
□ { 8 / 1

E
14 { 8 / □

F
□ { 5 / 2

5

```
 16       8      16       8      16       8      16       8
- 7      - 5     - 9     - 3     - 7     - 3     - 7     - 5
```

6

A	B	C	D	E
1035	2406	3006	5071	3401

Lesson 30 (continued)

7

A Ann had 9 oranges. She gave 4 oranges to her friends.

9 is a _____ _____ number.

4 is a _____ number.

B Jack has 7 books. He buys 2 books.

7 is a _____ number.

2 is a _____ number.

C Gloria has 4 pens. She gives away 1 pen.

4 is a _____ number.

1 is a _____ number.

D 6 children are in the park. 4 children go home.

6 is a _____ number.

4 is a _____ number.

E Roy ate 8 strawberries. Then he ate 5 more.

8 is a _____ number.

5 is a _____ number.

F Jane has 5 cats. 3 cats run away.

5 is a _____ number.

3 is a _____ number.

8

```
   A          B          C          D          E
  802        704       6084       8063        306
 -184       -553      -4191      -6153       - 48
```

9

```
   A          B          C          D          E
 7496       4825         90         70        420
-1895      +1362        +45        -45       -402


   F          G          H          I          J
 4826       7428       3245        528       9638
+ 850      -4357      - 724       +418       - 829
```

EXERCISE 1

Facts: Introducing Five Facts in Series

a. (Write on the board:)

$$7 \times 6 = 42$$
$$7 \times 7 = 49$$
$$7 \times 8 = 56$$
$$7 \times 9 = 63$$
$$7 \times 10 = 70$$

b. These are facts that start with 7. Let's read the facts together, starting with 7 times 6. Get ready. (Read the facts with the students. Signal.) *7 times 6 equals 42; 7 times 7 equals 49; 7 times 8 equals 56; 7 times 9 equals 63; 7 times 10 equals 70.*
- (Repeat step b until firm.)

c. (Erase the board.) Now say the facts without looking at them. Start with 7 times 6. Get ready.
- (Hold up six fingers. Signal.) *7 times 6 equals 42.*
- (Hold up seven fingers. Signal.) *7 times 7 equals 49.*
- (Hold up eight fingers. Signal.) *7 times 8 equals 56.*
- (Hold up nine fingers. Signal.) *7 times 9 equals 63.*
- (Hold up ten fingers. Signal.) *7 times 10 equals 70.*
- (Repeat step c until firm.)

d. (Call on individual students. Each student is to say the five facts in order.)

e. Open your workbook to Lesson 42. Find Part 1.

f. Touch the first problem. Read the problem and say the answer. (Signal.) *7 times 9 equals 63.*
- Touch the next problem. Read the problem and say the answer. (Signal.) *7 times 7 equals 49.*
- Touch the next problem. Read the problem and say the answer. (Signal.) *7 times 8 equals 56.*
- Touch the next problem. Read the problem and say the answer. (Signal.) *7 times 6 equals 42.*
- Touch the next problem. Read the problem and say the answer. (Signal.) *7 times 7 equals 49.*
- Touch the next problem. Read the problem and say the answer. (Signal.) *7 times 9 equals 63.*
- Touch the next problem. Read the problem and say the answer. (Signal.) *7 times 8 equals 56.*
- Touch the next problem. Read the problem and say the answer. (Signal.) *7 times 6 equals 42.*

g. (Repeat step f until firm.)

h. Write the answers to all the problems in Part 1. Get ready. Go.
- (Check and correct. See *Answer Key.*)

i. (Review answers orally with the entire group. See *Answer Key.*)

EXERCISE 2

Place Value: Practice Putting in Commas

a. Find Part 2 on your worksheet.

b. When you have a number with more than four digits, where do you write a comma? (Signal.) *Between the hundreds column and the thousands column.*

c. In Part 2, write a comma in each number that has more than four digits.
- (Check and correct. See *Answer Key.*)

d. Touch item A. (Pause.) Did you write a comma? (Signal.) *Yes.*
- How many thousands are there? (Signal.) *42.*
- Read item A. (Signal.) *Forty-two thousand thirty-eight.*

e. Touch item B. (Pause.) Did you write a comma? (Signal.) *No.*
- How many thousands are there? (Signal.) *7.*
- Read item B. (Signal.) *Seven thousand one hundred forty-nine.*

f. Touch item C. (Pause.) Did you write a comma? (Signal.) *Yes.*
- How many thousands are there? (Signal.) *30.*
- Read item C. (Signal.) *Thirty thousand eight hundred twenty.*

g. Touch item D. (Pause.) Did you write a comma? (Signal.) *Yes.*
- How many thousands are there? (Signal.) *41.*
- Read item D. (Signal.) *Forty-one thousand three hundred fifty-two.*

h. Touch item E. (Pause.) Did you write a comma? (Signal.) *No.*
- How many thousands are there? (Signal.) *7.*
- Read item E. (Signal.) *Seven thousand nine hundred four.*

EXERCISE 3

Operations: Which Box to Carry to

a. In the next lesson you're going to work problems that have more than two digits on top. You need to learn a new rule for carrying numbers to work these problems.

b. Find Part 3 on your worksheet.

c. Here's a rule for carrying numbers. The number you carry always goes in the box in front of the top number.

d. Look at problem A. Touch the 2. If you're multiplying the 2, you carry to the box in front of the 2. That's the box above the 5. Touch that box. ✔

e. Touch the 5. If you're multiplying the 5, you carry to the box in front of the 5. Touch that box. ✔
- What number is below that box? (Signal.) *3.*

f. Touch the 3. Now touch the box you'd carry to when you multiply the 3. What number is below that box? (Signal.) *8.*

g. Touch the 2 again. Now touch the box you'd carry to when you multiply the 2. What number is below that box? (Signal.) *5.*

h. Touch the 5. Now touch the box you'd carry to when you multiply the 5. What number is below that box? (Signal.) *3.*

i. Touch the 3. Now touch the box you'd carry to when you multiply the 3. What number is below that box? (Signal.) *8.*

New Problem

a. Look at problem B. Touch the 9. If you're multiplying the 9, you carry to the box in front of the 9. That's the box above the 2. Touch that box.

b. Touch the 2. If you're multiplying the 2, you carry to the box in front of the 2. Touch that box.
- What number is below that box? (Signal.) *8.*

c. Touch the 8. Now touch the box you'd carry to when you multiply the 8. What number is below that box? (Signal.) *4.*

d. Touch the 9. Now touch the box you'd carry to when you multiply the 9. What number is below that box? (Signal.) *2.*

e. Touch the 2 again. Now touch the box you'd carry to when you multiply the 2. What number is below that box? (Signal.) *8.*

f. Touch the 8. Now touch the box you'd carry to when you multiply the 8. What number is below that box? (Signal.) *4.*

EXERCISE 4

Facts: Practicing Carrying and Noncarrying Addition Preskills

a. I'm going to read some problems. You tell me the answers.

b. 30 (Pause.) 6 plus 3. Listen again. 36 plus 3. What's the answer? (Signal.) *39.*

c. 30 (Pause.) 6 plus 5. Listen again. 36 plus 5. What's the answer? (Signal.) *41.*

d. 50 (Pause.) 4 plus 6. Listen again. 54 plus 6. What's the answer? (Signal.) *60.*

e. 20 (Pause.) 8 plus 2. Listen again. 28 plus 2. What's the answer? (Signal.) *30.*

f. 40 (Pause.) 5 plus 3. Listen again. 45 plus 3. What's the answer? (Signal.) *48.*

g. 40 (Pause.) 8 plus 3. Listen again. 48 plus 3. What's the answer? (Signal.) *51.*

h. Find Part 4 on your worksheet. Now you're going to write the answers to the problems we just did. Don't write the problem, just the answer.

i. Problem A. 30 (Pause.) 6 plus 3. Listen again. 36 plus 3. Write the answer.

j. Problem B. 50 (Pause.) 4 plus 6. Listen again. 54 plus 6. Write the answer.

k. Problem C. 20 (Pause.) 8 plus 2. Listen again. 28 plus 2. Write the answer.

l. Problem D. 40 (Pause.) 5 plus 3. Listen again. 45 plus 3. Write the answer.

m. Problem E. 40 (Pause.) 8 plus 3. Listen again. 48 plus 3. Write the answer.

n. Problem F. 30 (Pause.) 6 plus 5. Listen again. 36 plus 5. Write the answer.

o. Let's check your work. I'll read the problems again. You say the answers you wrote.

p. Problem A. 36 plus 3. Everybody, what's the answer? (Signal.) *39.*

q. (Repeat step p for the rest of the problems in Part 4. See *Answer Key.*)

EXERCISE 5

Timing Format

a. Find Part 5 on your worksheet.

b. You're going to say the answers to some facts. Touch the first problem and get ready to tell me the answer. (Pause.) What's the answer? (Signal.) *24.*

c. Next problem. (Pause.) What's the answer? (Signal.) *35.*

d. (Repeat step c until firm for the rest of the problems in the first row. See *Answer Key.*)

e. Let's see how fast you can work these problems. You have one and a half minutes. Get ready. Go.

f. (After one and a half minutes say:) Stop. Put an **X** next to each problem you didn't get to.

g. Let's check your work. You're going to read each problem and say the answer. If you have the wrong answer, put an **X** next to the problem.

h. First problem. (Signal.) *8 times 3 equals 24.*

i. Next problem. (Signal.) *7 times 5 equals 35.*

j. (Repeat step i for the rest of the problems in Part 5. See *Answer Key.*)

EXERCISE 6

Facts: Practicing Commutative Property

a. Find Part 6 on your worksheet.

b. You're going to write two multiplication facts for each number family.

c. Touch number family A. What's the big number for that family? (Signal.) *24.*

• Write it in the box. ✔

d. Say the multiplication fact that begins with 6. (Signal.) *6 times 4 equals 24.*

e. Say the multiplication fact that begins with 4. (Signal.) *4 times 6 equals 24.*

f. Write both facts below number family A. ✔

g. Do the rest of the problems in Part 6 on your own. Fill in the big number for each family. Then write the two facts.

• (Check and correct. See *Answer Key.*)

h. Let's check your work. Put an **X** next to each fact you got wrong.

i. What's the big number for number family B? (Signal.) *12.*

• Say the multiplication fact that begins with 6. (Signal.) *6 times 2 equals 12.*

• Say the multiplication fact that begins with 2. (Signal.) *2 times 6 equals 12.*

j. What's the big number for number family C? (Signal.) *30.*

• Say the multiplication fact that begins with 6. (Signal.) *6 times 5 equals 30.*

• Say the multiplication fact that begins with 5. (Signal.) *5 times 6 equals 30.*

k. What's the big number for number family D?
(Signal.) *6.*
- Say the multiplication fact that begins with 6.
(Signal.) *6 times 1 equals 6.*
- Say the multiplication fact that begins with 1.
(Signal.) *1 times 6 equals 6.*

l. What's the big number for number family E?
(Signal.) *18.*
- Say the multiplication fact that begins with 6.
(Signal.) *6 times 3 equals 18.*
- Say the multiplication fact that begins with 3.
(Signal.) *3 times 6 equals 18.*

EXERCISE 7

Story Problems:
Introducing Subtraction Problems

a. Multiplication has number families. Addition and subtraction have number families too. Addition and subtraction number families have a big number and two small numbers. The big number is the number you end up with when you add the two small numbers. Today we're going to work addition, subtraction, and multiplication problems.

b. You already know how to tell whether a problem is a multiplication problem. Most multiplication problems use the word **each** or **every.** If a problem doesn't use the word **each** or **every,** it's probably an addition or subtraction problem.

c. Here are rules about addition and subtraction problems. If the big number is not given, it's an addition problem. If the big number is given, it's a subtraction problem.

d. Remember, when you add, you add only the two small numbers. When you subtract, you start with the big number and take away one of the small numbers.

e. What kind of problem is it if the word **each** or **every** is used? (Signal.) *Multiplication.*

f. Listen. I'll tell you about a problem. **Each** or **every** is not used in the problem and the big number is not given. What kind of problem is it? (Signal.) *Addition.*

To Correct
If the big number is not given, it's an addition problem.◄

g. Listen. I'll tell you about another problem. **Each** or **every** is not used and the big number is given. What kind of problem is it? (Signal.) *Subtraction.*

To Correct
If the big number is given, it's a subtraction problem.◄

h. (Repeat steps e–g until firm.)
i. Find Part 7 on your worksheet.
- I'll read story A. Katie Tallchief likes to take photographs of her classmates. She took 57 photographs. She gave 24 away. How many photographs did Katie have left?
j. Is the word **each** or **every** used? (Signal.) *No.*
- So it's not a multiplication problem. It's either an addition or subtraction problem.
k. Does the story give the big number? (Signal.) *Yes.*
- So what kind of problem is it? (Signal.) *Subtraction.*
l. Start with 57 and say the problem. (Signal.) *57 minus 24 equals how many?*

To Correct
The subtraction problem is 57 minus 24 equals how many?◄

m. Write the problem and figure the answer. ✔
n. I'll read story B. Mr. Singh buys 14 crates of lettuce for his restaurant each week. How many crates does he buy in 3 weeks?
o. Is the word **each** or **every** used? (Signal.) *Yes.*
- So what kind of problem is it? (Signal.) *Multiplication.*
p. Start with 14 and say the problem. (Signal.) *14 times 3.*
q. Write the problem and figure the answer. ✔
r. Work the rest of the problems in Part 7 on your own. Write each problem and figure the answer.

s. Let's check your work. Put an **X** next to any problems you got wrong.

t. Problem A. What's the answer? (Signal.) *33 photographs.*

u. Problem B. What's the answer? (Signal.) *42 crates.*

v. I'll read story C. A flower shop near a train station sold 14 bunches of daisies on Monday and 5 bunches on Tuesday. How many bunches did it sell in all?
- Read the problem and say the answer. (Signal.) *14 plus 5 equals 19 bunches.*

w. I'll read story D. In an art class, 22 students are working with clay and 5 are painting pictures. How many students in all are there in the art class?
- Read the problem and say the answer. (Signal.) *22 plus 5 equals 27 students.*

x. I'll read story E. Mrs. Arcano bought 14 pieces of wood to repair her porch. She needs 38 pieces of wood. How many more pieces does Mrs. Arcano need?
- Read the problem and say the answer. (Signal.) *38 minus 14 equals 24 pieces.*

EXERCISE 8

Preparation for Mastery Test: Facts

a. When we do the next lesson, you're going to have a test on multiplication facts. Let's go over some facts together.

b. I'll say the problems and you give the answers. What does 4 times 5 equal? Get ready. (Signal.) *20.*

c. (Repeat step b for the following problems: 4×6, 4×7, 4×8, 4×9, 4×5, 6×1, 6×2, 6×3, 6×4, 6×5)

d. Remember those facts for the test.

EXERCISE 9

Independent Work

Do Part 8. (The students can work this part without supervision.)

EXERCISE 10

Workcheck

a. Now we're going to figure out the number of points you earned for this lesson.

b. Count the number of facts you got wrong in Parts 5 and 6.

c. Find the beginning of your worksheet for Lesson 42.

d. If you got 0 or 1 wrong, you get 3 points. If you got 2 wrong, you get 1 point. If you got more than 2 wrong, you get 0 points.

e. Write the number of points you earned in the box labeled "Facts."

f. Now we'll check all of the problems in Part 8.

g. Put an **X** next to each problem you got wrong.

h. (Read the answers from the *Answer Key* for Lesson 42, Part 8.)

i. Now count the number of problems you got wrong in Parts 7 and 8.

j. Once again find the beginning of your worksheet for Lesson 42. You are going to write the number of points you earned in the box labeled "Problems."

k. If you got 0 or 1 wrong, you get 5 points. If you got 2 or 3 wrong, you get 3 points. If you got more than 3 wrong, you get 0 points.

l. Write the number of points you earned in the box labeled "Problems."

m. (If Fact Game bonus points are to be added to the "Bonus" box in this lesson, do not do steps n and o.)

n. Add up all of the points in the boxes and put the answer in the box labeled "Total." This is the number of points you earned for this lesson.

o. Turn to the Point Summary Charts on the inside back cover of your workbook. Find the empty box below Lesson 42. Write the total number of points you earned in that box.

Lesson 42

EXERCISE 11

Fact Game

a. (When you're ready to begin playing, divide the class into groups. Depending on the size of your class, there will be four or fewer students in each group plus a student who will be a judge. For each group you will need one die or spinner numbered from 1 through 6, a score sheet, and a pencil. Write the answers to the facts shown in step b on a blank sheet of paper. This paper will also serve as the group's score sheet.)

b. (Write the following facts on the board:)

1.	2.	3.	4.	5.	6.
4	4	4	4	7	7
×6	×7	×8	×9	×3	×4

c. (Give each team a die or spinner and give each judge a pencil and a sheet of paper with the answers to the facts.)

d. We're going to play a game called the Fact Game. You can earn up to 2 bonus points each day we play.

e. These are the rules of the game. All of the teams play the game at the same time. Each team starts by having one player roll the die or spin the spinner. The number that comes up tells which problem on the board that player must give the answer for. For example, if a 4 comes up on the spinner or die, you read problem 4, 4 times 9, and then give the answer. What do you do if a 2 comes up? (Signal.) *Read problem 2 and give the answer.*

f. If the answer is correct, the judge draws 1 line on the sheet of paper.

g. If the answer is incorrect, the judge crosses out 2 lines. (Be aware that when the first turn is taken, there will be no lines to cross out.)

h. How many lines does a judge draw for the correct answer? (Signal.) *1.*

- How many lines does a judge cross out for the wrong answer? (Signal.) *2.*

i. The players take turns answering the problems until I say "Stop." You will play for five minutes.

j. After I say "Stop," the judge will count up the team's lines.

k. (Pick a team and model the game for the rest of the students.) I'll play the game with this team. Everybody else should watch how we play.

l. (After you finish demonstrating the game, say:) When I signal, start playing. I'll tell you to stop at the end of five minutes. If you have any questions, raise your hand. (Signal.)

m. (Check each group during the game.)

n. (After five minutes are up, say:) Stop playing.

o. Judges, count the number of lines your team got and write the total at the top of your sheet of paper.

p. If your team got 30, 31, 32, 33, 34, 35, 36, 37, 38, or 39 lines, you get 1 point. If your team has 40 or more lines, you get 2 points. All judges get 2 points.

q. Write your points in the "Bonus" box at the beginning of your lesson for today. (Be aware that you might have already awarded some bonus points earlier in the lesson either for appropriate group behavior or for very good worksheet performance.)

r. (You might want to write numbers in the boxes on the board and demonstrate this next step.) Add up all of the points in the boxes and put the answer in the box labeled "Total." This is the number of points you earned for this lesson.

s. Turn to the Point Summary Charts on the inside back cover of your workbook. ✔ Find the empty box below Lesson 42. Write the total number of points you earned in that box. ✔

| Facts | + | Problems | + | Bonus | = | TOTAL |

1

7	7	7	7	7	7	7	7
×9	×7	×8	×6	×7	×9	×8	×6

7	7	7	7	7	7	7	7
×7	×9	×8	×7	×6	×9	×10	×8

2

A 42038   B 7149   C 30820   D 41352   E 7904

3

A

8 3 5 2
× 7 9

B

4 8 2 9
× 3 5

4

A _____ B _____ C _____ D _____ E _____ F _____

5

8	7	4	4	5	4	4	7
×3	×5	×8	×6	×7	×9	×7	×4

5	5	2	4	7	4	9	3
×6	×4	×8	×7	×3	×8	×4	×5

7	2	4	8	8	5	9	5
×2	×9	×0	×4	×2	×9	×2	×8

6

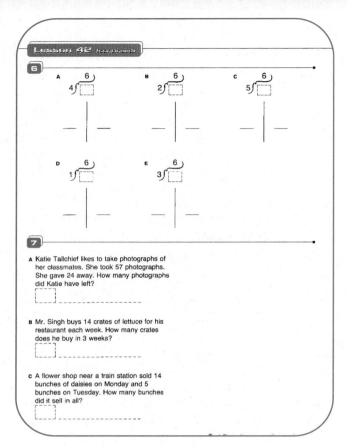

A 4)6̄   B 2)6̄   C 5)6̄

D 1)6̄   E 3)6̄

7

A Katie Tallchief likes to take photographs of her classmates. She took 57 photographs. She gave 24 away. How many photographs did Katie have left?

B Mr. Singh buys 14 crates of lettuce for his restaurant each week. How many crates does he buy in 3 weeks?

C A flower shop near a train station sold 14 bunches of daisies on Monday and 5 bunches on Tuesday. How many bunches did it sell in all?

D In an art class, 22 students are working with clay and 5 are painting pictures. How many students in all are there in the art class?

E Mrs. Arcano bought 14 pieces of wood to repair her porch. She needs 38 pieces of wood. How many more pieces does Mrs. Arcano need?

8

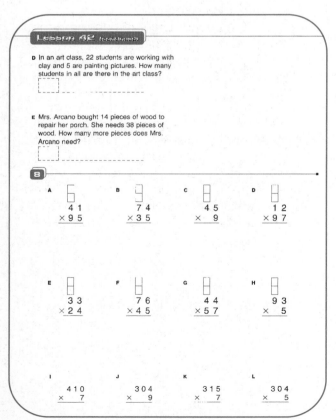

A	B	C	D
4 1	7 4	4 5	1 2
× 9 5	× 3 5	× 9	× 9 7

E	F	G	H
3 3	7 6	4 4	9 3
× 2 4	× 4 5	× 5 7	× 5

I	J	K	L
4 1 0	3 0 4	3 1 5	3 0 4
× 7	× 9	× 7	× 5

EXERCISE 1

Fact Review

a. Later you're going to work division problems. Let's review some facts for those problems.

b. 5 goes into 45 how many times? (Pause and signal.) *9.*

c. 5 goes into 30 how many times? (Pause and signal.) *6.*

d. 5 goes into 35 how many times? (Pause and signal.) *7.*

e. (Repeat steps b–d until firm.)

EXERCISE 2

Facts: Facts with Zeroes

a. Open your workbook to Lesson 21. Find Part 1.

• When you divide any number into zero, the answer is always zero.

b. Look at problem A. My turn. How many times does 7 go into zero? Zero. How do you know? 7 times zero equals zero.

c. Look at problem B. My turn. How many times does 2 go into zero? Zero. How do you know? 2 times zero equals zero.

d. Look at problem C. Your turn. How many times does 9 go into zero? (Signal.) *Zero.*

• How do you know? (Signal.) *9 times zero equals zero.*

e. Look at problem D. How many times does 5 go into zero? (Signal.) *Zero.*

• How do you know? (Signal.) *5 times zero equals zero.*

f. Look at problem E. Your turn. How many times does 3 go into zero? (Signal.) *Zero.*

• How do you know? (Signal.) *3 times zero equals zero.*

EXERCISE 3

Facts: Writing Division Problems from Dictation

a. Find Part 2 on your worksheet. I'll read some division problems. You write them.

b. Problem A. 5 goes into 35. Say the problem. (Signal.) *5 goes into 35.*

• Write it. Don't work it yet. ✔

c. Problem B. 5 goes into 30. Say the problem. (Signal.) *5 goes into 30.*

• Write it. ✔

d. Problem C. 5 goes into 45. Say the problem. (Signal.) *5 goes into 45.*

• Write it. ✔

e. Problem D. 5 goes into 40. Say the problem. (Signal.) *5 goes into 40.*

• Write it. ✔

f. Now write the answers to those problems.

• (Check and correct. See *Answer Key*.)

g. (Review answers orally with the entire group.)

EXERCISE 4

Reading Digits

a. Find Part 3 on your worksheet.

b. Touch problem A. ✔

• It says 5 goes into 6 hundred 38.

c. My turn to read the first digit in 6 hundred 38. (Pause.) 6.

• My turn to read the first two digits in 6 hundred 38. (Pause.) 63.

d. Touch problem B. ✔

• We're dividing 5 into 4 thousand 6 hundred 27. Your turn to read the first digit in 4 thousand 6 hundred 27. (Signal.) *4.*

• Your turn to read the first two digits in 4 thousand 6 hundred 27. (Signal.) *46.*

e. Look at problem C. We're dividing 5 into 5 hundred 32. Your turn to read the first digit in 5 hundred 32. (Signal.) *5.*

• Your turn to read the first two digits in 5 hundred 32. (Signal.) *53.*

f. (Call on individual students. Each student is to read the first two digits of problems A–D.)

EXERCISE 5

Operations: Underlining Rule for Working Problems

a. (Continue with worksheet Part 3.) In problems A, B, and C, we're dividing 5 into a number with many digits. You have to figure out how many of the digits to use. Here's the rule. If the first digit is at least as big as 5, you underline the first digit. If the first digit in not as big as 5, you underline the first two digits.

b. Look at problem A again. It says that 5 goes into 6 hundred 38. Read the first digit we're dividing 5 into. (Signal.) *6.*
- Is 6 at least as big as 5? (Signal.) *Yes.*
- So underline the 6. ✔

c. Look at problem B. It says that 5 goes into 4 thousand 6 hundred 27. What's the first digit we're dividing 5 into? (Signal.) *4.*
- Is 4 at least as big as 5? (Signal.) *No.*
- So underline the first two digits. Read the first two digits. (Signal.) *46.*
- 46 is at least as big as 5. Underline 46. ✔

d. Look at problem C. It says that 5 goes into 5 hundred 32. What's the first digit we're dividing 5 into? (Signal.) *5.*
- Is 5 at least as big as 5? (Signal.) *Yes.*
- So what are you going to underline? (Signal.) *5.*
- Underline it. ✔

e. I'll read the underlined problem. 5 goes into 5. Now you read the underlined problem. (Signal.) *5 goes into 5.*

f. (Repeat steps b–e until firm.)

g. Now we're going to divide 9 into a number. Look at problem D. What does problem D say? (Signal.) *9 goes into 4 hundred 67.*
- What's the first digit we're dividing 9 into? (Signal.) *4.*
- Is 4 at least as big as 9? (Signal.) *No.*
- So what are you going to underline? (Signal.) *46.*
- (Repeat all steps in g until firm.)
- Underline 46. ✔

h. I'll read the underlined problem. 9 goes into 46. Now you read the underlined problem. (Signal.) *9 goes into 46.*

EXERCISE 6

Operations: Writing the Answer Above the Last Underlined Digit

a. (Continue with worksheet Part 3.) Look at problem D again. When you work this kind of problem, you start writing your answer above the last digit you underlined. What's the **last** digit you underlined? (Signal.) *6.*
- So you're going to start writing your answer right above the 6.

b. What does the underlined problem say? (Signal.) *9 goes into 46.*

c. What number did you write above the 6? (Signal.) *5.*

d. What number does 9 go into 5 times without a remainder? (Signal.) *45.*
- Write 45 below 46 and subtract. ✔

e. What's the remainder for the underlined problem? (Signal.) *1.*

f. Work the underlined part of the other problems on your own. Remember to write your answer above the last digit you underlined.
- (Check and correct. See *Answer Key.*)

g. (Review answers orally with the entire group.)

EXERCISE 7

Story Problems: Practice

a. Find Part 4 on your worksheet.

b. Write the problems for the stories in Part 4, but don't work the problems. Just write them.
- (Check and correct. See *Answer Key.* Make sure the students write the problems beside the story and not on the line next to the box.)

c. (Review answers orally with the entire group.)

EXERCISE 8

Story Problems: Writing a Word as Part of the Answer

a. (Continue with worksheet Part 4.) You're going to write the word that is part of the answer. I'll work some problems with you.
- Problem A. A student used 3 papers every lesson. She did 50 lessons. How many papers did the student use?

b. What does problem A want us to find out? (Signal.) *How many papers the student used.*
- So the word that is part of the answer is **papers.** Write **papers** on the line below problem A.

c. Problem B. A seal balanced 5 balls in every show. It balanced 40 balls in shows. How many times was the seal in a show?

d. What does problem B want us to find out? (Signal.) *How many times the seal was in a show.*
- What word is part of the answer? (Signal.) *Times.*
- Write **times** on the line below problem B.

e. Problem C. Judy worked 3 hours every day. She worked 60 days. How many hours did Judy work?

f. What does problem C want us to find out? (Signal.) *How many hours Judy worked.*
- What word is part of the answer? (Signal.) *Hours.*
- Write **hours** on the line below problem C.

g. Write the word that is part of the answer on the line below the rest of the problems in Part 3.
- (Check and correct. See *Answer Key.*)

h. I'll read problem A again. A student used 3 papers every lesson. She did 50 lessons. How many papers did the student use?

i. Is the big number given in this problem? (Signal.) *No.*
- So what kind of problem is it? (Signal.) *Multiplication.*

j. Work the problem and figure the answer. Then copy the answer in the box. ✔

k. The story problem asks: How many papers did the student use? Everybody, say the whole answer. (Signal.) *150 papers.*

l. Work the rest of the problems in Part 4 on your own. Figure out the answers and then copy the answers in the box.
- (Check and correct. See *Answer Key.*)

m. (Review answers orally with the entire group.)

EXERCISE 9

Preparation for Mastery Test: Facts

a. When we do the next lesson, you're going to have a test on division facts. Let's go over some facts together.

b. I'll say the problems and you give the answers. 3 goes into 15 how many times? Get ready. (Signal.) *5.*

c. (Repeat step b for the following problems:)

$5\overline{)20}$	$3\overline{)6}$	$5\overline{)25}$	$9\overline{)36}$
$3\overline{)12}$	$9\overline{)18}$	$3\overline{)9}$	$9\overline{)45}$

d. Remember those facts for the test.

EXERCISE 10

Timing Format

a. Find Part 5 on your worksheet.

b. See how fast you can work these problems. You have one and a half minutes. Get ready. Go.
- (After one and a half minutes, say:) Stop.

c. Put an **X** next to each problem you didn't finish. Now let's check the problems.

d. You're going to read each problem and say the answer. If you have the wrong answer, put an **X** next to the problem. Get ready. Go.

EXERCISE 11

Independent Work

- Do Parts 6 and 7. (The students can work these parts without supervision.)

EXERCISE 12

Workcheck

a. Count the number of facts you got wrong in Part 5.

b. Find the beginning of your worksheet for Lesson 21.

c. If you got 0, 1, or 2 wrong, you get 3 points. If you got 3 wrong, you get 1 point. If you got more than 3 wrong, you get 0 points.

d. Write the number of points you earned in the box labeled "Facts."

e. Now we'll check all of the problems in Parts 6 and 7.

f. (Read the answers from the *Answer Key* for Lesson 21, Parts 6 and 7.)

g. Find again find the beginning of your worksheet for Lesson 21.

h. If you got 0, 1, or 2 wrong, you get 5 points. If you got 3 or 4 wrong, you get 3 points. If you got more than 4 wrong, you get 0 points.

i. Write the number of points you earned in the box labeled "Problems."

j. (If Fact Game bonus points are to be added to the "Bonus" box in this lesson, do not do steps k and l.)

k. Add up all the points in the boxes and put the answer in the box labeled "Total." These are the number of points you earned for this lesson.

l. Turn to the Point Summary Charts on the inside back cover of your workbook. Find the empty box below Lesson 21. Write the total number of points you earned in that box.

EXERCISE 13

Fact Game

a. (When you're ready to begin playing, divide the class into groups. Depending on the size of your class, there will be four or fewer students in each group plus a student who will be judge. For each group you will need one die or spinner numbered from 1 through 6, a score sheet, and a pencil. Write the answers to the facts shown in step b on a blank sheet of paper. This paper will also serve as the group's score sheet.)

b. (Write the following problems on the board:)

1. $5\overline{)5}$	2. $5\overline{)10}$	3. $5\overline{)15}$
4. $5\overline{)20}$	5. $1\overline{)7}$	6. $1\overline{)6}$

c. (Give each team a die or spinner and give each judge a pencil and a sheet of paper with the answers.)

d. We're going to play a game called the Fact Game. You can earn up to 2 bonus points each day we play.

e. These are the rules of the game. All of the teams play the game at the same time. Each team starts by having one player roll the die or spin the spinner. The number that comes up tells which problem on the board that player must give the answer for. For example, if a 4 comes up on the spinner or die, you read problem 4, 5 goes into 20, and then give the answer. What do you do if a 2 comes up? (Signal.) *Read problem 2 and give the answer.*

f. If the answer is correct, the judge draws one line on the sheet of paper.

g. If the answer is incorrect, the judge crosses out two lines. (Be aware that when the first turn is taken there will be no lines to cross out.)

h. How many lines does a judge draw for the correct answer? (Signal.) *One.*

• How many lines does a judge cross out for the wrong answer? (Signal.) *Two.*

i. Take turns answering the problems until I say "Stop." You will play for five minutes.

j. After I say "Stop," the judge will count up the team's lines.

k. (Pick a team and model the game for the rest of the students.) I'll play the game with this team. Everybody else should watch how we play.

l. (After you finish demonstrating the game, say:) When I signal, start playing. I'll tell you to stop at the end of five minutes. If you have any questions, raise your hand. (Signal.)

m. (Check each group during the game.)

n. (After five minutes are up, say:) Stop playing.

o. Judges, count the number of lines the team got and write the total at the top of the sheet of paper.

p. If your team got 30, 31, 32, 33, 34, 35, 36, 37, 38, or 39 lines, you get 1 point. If your team has 40 or more lines, you get 2 points. All judges get 2 points.

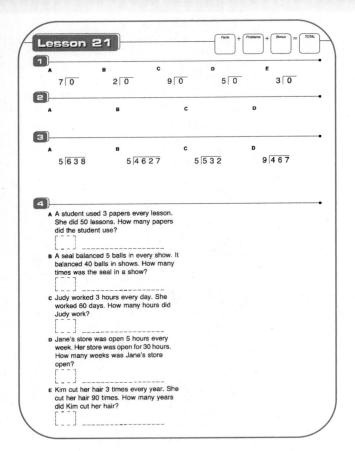

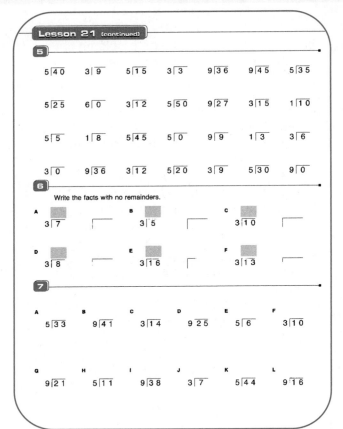

Lesson 21

Facts + Problems + Bonus = TOTAL

1

A $7\overline{)0}$ B $2\overline{)0}$ C $9\overline{)0}$ D $5\overline{)0}$ E $3\overline{)0}$

2

A   B   C   D

3

A $5\overline{)638}$ B $5\overline{)4627}$ C $5\overline{)532}$ D $9\overline{)467}$

4

A A student used 3 papers every lesson. She did 50 lessons. How many papers did the student use?

B A seal balanced 5 balls in every show. It balanced 40 balls in shows. How many times was the seal in a show?

C Judy worked 3 hours every day. She worked 60 days. How many hours did Judy work?

D Jane's store was open 5 hours every week. Her store was open for 30 hours. How many weeks was Jane's store open?

E Kim cut her hair 3 times every year. She cut her hair 90 times. How many years did Kim cut her hair?

Lesson 21 (continued)

5

$5\overline{)40}$ $3\overline{)9}$ $5\overline{)15}$ $3\overline{)3}$ $9\overline{)36}$ $9\overline{)45}$ $5\overline{)35}$

$5\overline{)25}$ $6\overline{)0}$ $3\overline{)12}$ $5\overline{)50}$ $9\overline{)27}$ $3\overline{)15}$ $1\overline{)10}$

$5\overline{)5}$ $1\overline{)8}$ $5\overline{)45}$ $5\overline{)0}$ $9\overline{)9}$ $1\overline{)3}$ $3\overline{)6}$

$3\overline{)0}$ $9\overline{)36}$ $3\overline{)12}$ $5\overline{)20}$ $3\overline{)9}$ $5\overline{)30}$ $9\overline{)0}$

6

Write the facts with no remainders.

A $3\overline{)7}$ B $3\overline{)5}$ C $3\overline{)10}$

D $3\overline{)8}$ E $3\overline{)16}$ F $3\overline{)13}$

7

A $5\overline{)33}$ B $9\overline{)41}$ C $3\overline{)14}$ D $9\overline{)25}$ E $5\overline{)6}$ F $3\overline{)10}$

G $9\overline{)21}$ H $5\overline{)11}$ I $9\overline{)38}$ J $3\overline{)7}$ K $5\overline{)44}$ L $9\overline{)16}$

EXERCISE 1

Multiplication/Addition/ Subtraction

a. Turn to Lesson 33.
 • Look at the problems in Part 1.
 • In some of these problems, you add or subtract. In some of the problems, you multiply.

b. When you add or subtract, you have to be able to rewrite the problem. When you multiply, you multiply top times the top and bottom times the bottom.
 • First I want you to tell me whether the problem is the kind you can rewrite to add or subtract or the kind you multiply top times the top and bottom times the bottom.

c. Touch the first problem.
 • Do you rewrite to add or subtract or do you multiply top times the top and bottom times the bottom? (Signal.) *Rewrite to add or subtract.*

d. Touch the next problem.
 • Do you rewrite to add or subtract or do you multiply top times the top and bottom times the bottom? (Signal.) *Rewrite to add or subtract.*

e. Touch the next problem.
 • Do you rewrite to add or subtract or do you multiply top times the top and bottom times the bottom? (Signal.) *Multiply top times the top and bottom times the bottom.*

f. Work all of the problems in Part 1. If the problem is the kind you can rewrite to add or subtract, work it the fast way. Remember to write the line in the answer. You have 7 minutes.
 • (Observe students and give feedback.)

EXERCISE 2

Addition/Subtraction

a. (Write on the board:)
★

$$\frac{2}{3} + \frac{5}{3} \qquad \frac{8}{7} - \frac{3}{8} \qquad \frac{9}{6} - \frac{4}{6} \qquad \frac{6}{7} + \frac{3}{7}$$

b. When can you add or subtract fractions? (Signal.) *When the wholes are the same.*
 • We're going to learn to add and subtract fractions when they are written like this.

c. I'll point and you read the problem.
 • (Touch each part as the students read.) *2 thirds plus 5 thirds.*
 • You can add those fractions the way they are because the wholes are the same.

d. What will I write on the bottom for the answer? (Signal.) *3.*
 • (Write to show:)

$$\frac{2}{3} + \frac{5}{3} = \frac{}{3} \qquad \frac{8}{7} - \frac{3}{8} \qquad \frac{9}{6} - \frac{4}{6} \qquad \frac{6}{7} + \frac{3}{7}$$

 • The top is 2 plus 5. What does that equal? (Signal.) *7.*
 • I'll write that in for the top of the answer.
 • (Write to show:)

$$\frac{2}{3} + \frac{5}{3} = \frac{7}{3} \qquad \frac{8}{7} - \frac{3}{8} \qquad \frac{9}{6} - \frac{4}{6} \qquad \frac{6}{7} + \frac{3}{7}$$

 • Tell me the whole answer to the problem. (Signal.) *7 thirds.*

e. Read the next problem.
- (Touch each part as the students read.) *8 sevenths minus 3 eighths.*
- Can we subtract these fractions the way they are? (Signal.) *No.*
- Why not? (Signal.) *The wholes aren't the same.*

f. Read the next problem.
- (Touch each part as the students read.) *9 sixths minus 4 sixths.*
- Can we subtract these fractions the way they are? (Signal.) *Yes.*
- You can subtract those fractions the way they are because the wholes are the same.

g. What will I write on the bottom for the answer? (Signal.) *6.*
- (Write to show:)

$$+\frac{2}{3}\frac{5}{3} \qquad -\frac{8}{7}\frac{3}{8} \qquad -\frac{9}{6}\frac{4}{6} \qquad +\frac{6}{7}\frac{3}{7}$$
$$\frac{7}{3} \qquad\qquad\qquad \frac{}{6}$$

- The top is 9 minus 4. What does that equal? (Signal.) *5.*
- I'll write that in for the top of the answer.
- (Write to show:)

$$+\frac{2}{3}\frac{5}{3} \qquad -\frac{8}{7}\frac{3}{8} \qquad -\frac{9}{6}\frac{4}{6} \qquad +\frac{6}{7}\frac{3}{7}$$
$$\frac{7}{3} \qquad\qquad\qquad \frac{5}{6}$$

- Tell me the whole answer to the problem. (Signal.) *5 sixths.*

h. Read the last problem.
- (Touch each part as the students read.) *6 sevenths plus 3 sevenths.*
- Can we add these fractions the way they are? (Signal.) *Yes.*
- You can add those fractions the way they are because the wholes are the same.

i. What will I write on the bottom for the answer? (Signal.) *7.*
- (Write to show:)

$$+\frac{2}{3}\frac{5}{3} \qquad -\frac{8}{7}\frac{3}{8} \qquad -\frac{9}{6}\frac{4}{6} \qquad +\frac{6}{7}\frac{3}{7}$$
$$\frac{7}{3} \qquad\qquad\qquad \frac{5}{6} \qquad \frac{}{7}$$

- The top is 6 plus 3. What does that equal? (Signal.) *9.*
- I'll write that in for the top of the answer.
- (Write to show:)

$$+\frac{2}{3}\frac{5}{3} \qquad -\frac{8}{7}\frac{3}{8} \qquad -\frac{9}{6}\frac{4}{6} \qquad +\frac{6}{7}\frac{3}{7}$$
$$\frac{7}{3} \qquad\qquad\qquad \frac{5}{6} \qquad \frac{9}{7}$$

- Tell me the whole answer to the problem. (Signal.) *9 sevenths.*

j. Look at the problems in Part 2. Figure out the answers to all of the problems you can work. Skip the problems you can't work. You have 3 minutes.
- (Observe students and give feedback.)

EXERCISE 3

Workcheck

a. We're going to check the answers. Exchange workbooks, and get ready to check the answers. (Pause.)

• Put an **X** next to each problem that the person misses.

• (Check and correct. See **Answer Key.**)

• Return the workbooks.

b. Now we're going to figure out the number of points you've earned for this lesson.

• (Point to the posted information.)

Worksheet Items	Errors	Points
	0–2	10
	3	7
	4	5
	5	3
	6	1
	7 or more	0

• Count the number of items you got wrong. Figure out the number of points you earned and write the number in the "Items" box.

• (Observe students and give feedback.)

c. (Tell the group how many points they earned for the lesson.) Write that number in the "Hard Work" box; then figure out the total for today's lesson.

d. Turn to the Point Summary Charts. Write the points in the box for Lesson 33. ✔

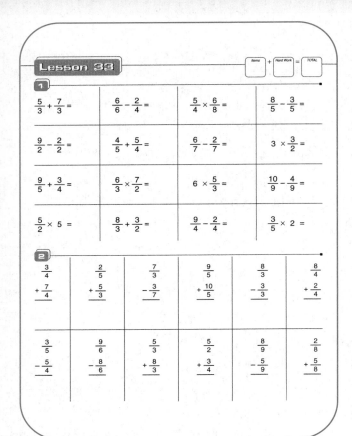

Lesson 33

Items + Hard Work = TOTAL

1

$\frac{5}{3} + \frac{7}{3} =$	$\frac{6}{6} - \frac{2}{4} =$	$\frac{5}{4} \times \frac{6}{8} =$	$\frac{8}{5} - \frac{3}{5} =$
$\frac{9}{2} - \frac{2}{2} =$	$\frac{4}{5} + \frac{5}{4} =$	$\frac{6}{7} - \frac{2}{7} =$	$3 \times \frac{3}{2} =$
$\frac{9}{5} + \frac{3}{4} =$	$\frac{6}{3} \times \frac{7}{2} =$	$6 \times \frac{5}{3} =$	$\frac{10}{9} - \frac{4}{9} =$
$\frac{5}{2} \times 5 =$	$\frac{8}{3} + \frac{3}{2} =$	$\frac{9}{4} - \frac{2}{4} =$	$\frac{3}{5} \times 2 =$

2

| $\frac{3}{4}$ $+ \frac{7}{4}$ | $\frac{2}{5}$ $+ \frac{5}{3}$ | $\frac{7}{3}$ $- \frac{3}{7}$ | $\frac{9}{5}$ $+ \frac{10}{5}$ | $\frac{8}{3}$ $- \frac{3}{3}$ | $\frac{8}{4}$ $+ \frac{2}{4}$ |
| $\frac{3}{5}$ $- \frac{5}{4}$ | $\frac{9}{6}$ $- \frac{8}{6}$ | $\frac{5}{3}$ $+ \frac{8}{3}$ | $\frac{5}{2}$ $+ \frac{3}{4}$ | $\frac{8}{9}$ $- \frac{5}{9}$ | $\frac{2}{8}$ $+ \frac{5}{8}$ |

Point Summary Charts

1.

Lesson	1	2	3	4	5	Total
Points						

2.

Lesson	6	7	8	9	10	Total
Points						

3.

Lesson	11	12	13	14	15	Total
Points						

4.

Lesson	16	17	18	19	20	Total
Points						

5.

Lesson	21	22	23	24	25	Total
Points						

6.

Lesson	26	27	28	29	30	Total
Points						

7.

Lesson	31	32	33	34	35	Total
Points						

8.

Lesson	36	37	38	39	40	Total
Points						

9.

Lesson	41	42	43	44	45	Total
Points						

10.

Lesson	46	47	48	49	50	Total
Points						

11.

Lesson	51	52	53	54	55	Total
Points						

A grade: The average of five-lesson totals is at least 50 points.
B grade: The average of five-lesson totals is 40–49 points.
C grade: The average of five-lesson totals is 30–39 points.
An average of five-lesson totals of less than 30 points is a failing grade for this course.

Daily Points

Daily points will be awarded by the teacher as follows:

1. Worksheet Items

Errors	Points
0–2	10
3	7
4	5
5	3
6	1
7 or more	0

2. Hard Work — 0–5 group points for working hard and answering on signal. Everyone in the group will receive the same number of points for oral work.

EXERCISE 1

Dividing Fractions

a. Open your workbook to Lesson 5.
- Touch the first problem in Part 1.
- It tells you to turn the fraction into 1. How do you change a fraction into 1? (Signal.) *Turn the fraction upside down and multiply.*

b. Do all the problems in Part 1. Turn each fraction into 1. You have 3 minutes.
- (Observe students and give feedback.)

EXERCISE 2

Reducing Fractions

a. Look at Part 2. Find the biggest number you can multiply by to reach both of the numbers in the pairs in Part 2.

b. You have 3 minutes.
- (Observe students and give feedback.)

EXERCISE 3

Reducing Fractions

a. (Write on the board:)

$$\frac{6}{9}$$

- We're going to reduce this fraction by taking out the biggest fraction equal to 1. What do we take out to reduce a fraction? (Signal.) *The biggest fraction equal to 1.*
- Let's reduce 6 ninths. To find the biggest fraction equal to 1, we have to find the biggest number we can multiply by to reach 6 and 9.
- Figure out the biggest number we can multiply by to reach 6 and 9. (Pause.)
- What's the answer? (Signal.) *3.*
- If 3 is the biggest number we can multiply by to reach 6 and 9, the biggest fraction equal to 1 we can take out is 3 thirds.

- (Write to show:)

$$\frac{6}{9} = \left(\frac{3}{3}\right) \times -$$

b. Let's figure out the top of the reduced fraction.
- (Point as you read:)
- 6 equals 3 times what number? (Signal.) *2.*
- (Write to show:)

$$\frac{6}{9} = \left(\frac{3}{3}\right) \times \frac{2}{-}$$

- Let's figure out the bottom.
- (Point as you read:)
- 9 equals 3 times what number? (Signal.) *3.*
- (Write to show:)

$$\frac{6}{9} = \left(\frac{3}{3}\right) \times \frac{2}{3}$$

c. The fraction in parentheses equals 1, so we can cross it out.

- (Cross out $\left(\frac{3}{3}\right)$.)
- When we take out the fraction equal to 1, the reduced fraction is 2 thirds. What's the reduced fraction? (Signal.) *2 thirds.*
- (Write to show:)

$$\frac{6}{9} = \left(\frac{\cancel{3}}{\cancel{3}}\right) \times \frac{2}{3} = \frac{2}{3}$$

d. Let's do another one.
- (Write on the board:)

$$\frac{4}{12}$$

- What do we take out to reduce a fraction? (Signal.) *The biggest fraction equal to 1.*
- To find the biggest fraction equal to 1, we have to find the biggest number we can multiply by to reach 4 and 12.
- Tell me the biggest number we can multiply by. (Pause.) (Signal.) *4.*

- If 4 is the biggest number we can multiply by. The biggest fraction equal to 1 we can take out is 4 fourths.
- (Write to show:)

$$\frac{4}{12} = \left(\frac{4}{4}\right) \times \underline{}$$

e. Figure out the top of the reduced fraction. (Pause.)
- What is the top? (Signal.) *1.*
- (Write to show:)

$$\frac{4}{12} = \left(\frac{4}{4}\right) \times \frac{1}{}$$

- Figure out the bottom of the reduced fraction. (Pause.)
- What is the bottom? (Signal.) *3.*
- (Write to show:)

$$\frac{4}{12} = \left(\frac{4}{4}\right) \times \frac{1}{3}$$

- The fraction in parentheses equals 1, so we can cross it out.
- (Cross out $\left(\frac{4}{4}\right)$.)
- When we take out the fraction equal to 1, what is the reduced fraction? (Signal.) *1 third.*
- (Write to show:)

$$\frac{4}{12} = \left(\cancel{\frac{4}{4}}\right) \times \frac{1}{3} = \frac{1}{3}$$

f. Let's reduce one more.
- (Write on the board:)

$$\frac{10}{6}$$

- What do we take out to reduce a fraction? (Signal.) *The biggest fraction equal to 1.*
- To find the biggest fraction equal to 1, we have to find the biggest number we can multiply by to reach 10 and 6.

- Tell me the biggest number we can multiply by. (Pause.) (Signal.) *2.*
- If 2 is the biggest number we can multiply by, the biggest fraction equal to 1 we can take out is 2 halves.
- (Write to show:)

$$\frac{10}{6} = \left(\frac{2}{2}\right) \times \underline{}$$

- Figure out the top of the reduced fraction. (Pause.)
- What is the top? (Signal.) *5.*

g. (Write to show:)

$$\frac{10}{6} = \left(\frac{2}{2}\right) \times \frac{5}{}$$

- Figure out the bottom of the reduced fraction. (Pause.)
- What is the bottom? (Signal.) *3.*

h. (Write to show:)

$$\frac{10}{6} = \left(\frac{2}{2}\right) \times \frac{5}{3}$$

- The fraction in the parentheses equals 1, so we can cross it out.
- (Cross out $\left(\frac{2}{2}\right)$.)
- When we take out the fraction equal to 1, what is the reduced fraction? (Signal.) *5 thirds.*
- (Write to show:)

$$\frac{10}{6} = \left(\frac{2}{2}\right) \times \frac{5}{3} = \frac{5}{3}$$

EXERCISE 4

Addition/Subtraction

a. (Write on the board:)

★

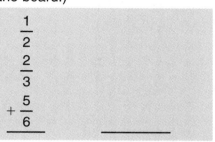

$$\begin{array}{r} \dfrac{1}{2} \\[4pt] \dfrac{2}{3} \\[4pt] +\dfrac{5}{6} \\ \hline \end{array}$$

- Can we work this problem the way it is? (Signal.) *No.*
- Why not? (Signal.) *The wholes aren't the same.*
- To make the wholes the same, we have to make a new bottom number. How do we make a new bottom number? (Signal.) *Multiply the old bottoms together.*
- Tell me the numbers for the new bottom. (Pause.) (Signal.) *2 times 3 times 6.*
- (Write the new bottoms.)

$$\begin{array}{r} \dfrac{1}{2} = \dfrac{}{2 \times 3 \times 6} \\[10pt] \dfrac{2}{3} = \dfrac{}{2 \times 3 \times 6} \\[10pt] +\dfrac{5}{6} = \dfrac{}{2 \times 3 \times 6} \\ \hline \end{array}$$

b. In the new fractions, we want to end with the same amount we start with, so what will we multiply by? (Signal.) *1.*
- Let's figure out the fractions equal to 1. What's the new bottom number of 1 half going to be? (Signal.) *2 times 3 times 6.*
- What's the old bottom of 1 half? (signal.) *2.*
- So what do we have to multiply the 2 by? (Signal.) *3 times 6.*
- So what fraction that equals 1 do we multiply by? (Signal.) *3 times 6 over 3 times 6.*

- (Write to show:)

$$\begin{array}{r} \dfrac{1}{2}\left(\dfrac{3 \times 6}{3 \times 6}\right) = \dfrac{}{2 \times 3 \times 6} \\[10pt] \dfrac{2}{3} = \dfrac{}{2 \times 3 \times 6} \\[10pt] +\dfrac{5}{6} = \dfrac{}{2 \times 3 \times 6} \\ \hline \end{array}$$

- What's the new bottom of 2 thirds going to be? (Signal.) *2 times 3 times 6.*
- What's the old bottom of 2 thirds? (Signal.) *3.*
- So what do we have to multiply the 3 by? (Signal.) *2 times 6.*
- So what fraction that equals 1 do we multiply by? (Signal.) *2 times 6 over 2 times 6.*
- (Write to show:)

$$\begin{array}{r} \dfrac{1}{2}\left(\dfrac{3 \times 6}{3 \times 6}\right) = \dfrac{}{2 \times 3 \times 6} \\[10pt] \dfrac{2}{3}\left(\dfrac{2 \times 6}{2 \times 6}\right) = \dfrac{}{2 \times 3 \times 6} \\[10pt] +\dfrac{5}{6} = \dfrac{}{2 \times 3 \times 6} \\ \hline \end{array}$$

- What's the new bottom of 5 sixths going to be? (Signal.) *2 times 3 times 6.*
- What's the old bottom of 5 sixths? (Signal.) *6.*
- So what do we have to multiply the 6 by? (Signal.) *2 times 3.*
- So what fraction that equals 1 do we multiply by? (Signal.) *2 times 3 over 2 times 3.*

- (Write to show:)

$$\frac{1}{2}\left(\frac{3\times6}{3\times6}\right)=\frac{}{2\times3\times6}$$

$$\frac{2}{3}\left(\frac{2\times6}{2\times6}\right)=\frac{}{2\times3\times6}$$

$$+\frac{5}{6}\left(\frac{2\times3}{2\times3}\right)=\frac{}{2\times3\times6}$$

c. Let's figure out the new top numbers for each fraction. Read the numbers you multiply for the new top number of the first fraction. (**Signal.**) *1 times 3 times 6.*
- Tell me what that equals. (**Pause.**) (**Signal.**) *18.*
- (Write to show:)

$$\frac{1}{2}\left(\frac{3\times6}{3\times6}\right)=\frac{18}{2\times3\times6}$$

$$\frac{2}{3}\left(\frac{2\times6}{2\times6}\right)=\frac{}{2\times3\times6}$$

$$+\frac{5}{6}\left(\frac{2\times3}{2\times3}\right)=\frac{}{2\times3\times6}$$

- Read the numbers you multiply for the top number in the next fraction. (**Signal.**) *2 times 2 times 6.*
- Tell me what that equals. (**Pause.**) (**Signal.**) *24.*
- (Write to show:)

$$\frac{1}{2}\left(\frac{3\times6}{3\times6}\right)=\frac{18}{2\times3\times6}$$

$$\frac{2}{3}\left(\frac{2\times6}{2\times6}\right)=\frac{24}{2\times3\times6}$$

$$+\frac{5}{6}\left(\frac{2\times3}{2\times3}\right)=\frac{}{2\times3\times6}$$

- Read the numbers you multiply for the top number in the next fraction. (**Signal.**) 5 *times 2 times 3.*
- Tell me what that equals. (**Pause.**) (**Signal.**) *30.*
- (Write to show:)

$$\frac{1}{2}\left(\frac{3\times6}{3\times6}\right)=\frac{18}{2\times3\times6}$$

$$\frac{2}{3}\left(\frac{2\times6}{2\times6}\right)=\frac{24}{2\times3\times6}$$

$$+\frac{5}{6}\left(\frac{2\times3}{2\times3}\right)=\frac{30}{2\times3\times6}$$

d. Read the numbers you multiply for the new bottom number. (**Signal.**) *2 times 3 times 6.*
- Tell me what that equals. (**Pause.**) (**Signal.**) *36.*
- I'll take those out and write the new bottom number for each fraction.
- (Cross out the 2 × 3 × 6 and write 36 for each fraction.)
- What's the bottom for the answer? (**Signal.**) *36.*
- (Write under the bottom line:)

$$\frac{1}{2}\left(\frac{3\times6}{3\times6}\right)=\frac{18}{\cancel{2\times3\times6}\ 36}$$

$$\frac{2}{3}\left(\frac{2\times6}{2\times6}\right)=\frac{24}{\cancel{2\times3\times6}\ 36}$$

$$+\frac{5}{6}\left(\frac{2\times3}{2\times3}\right)=\frac{30}{\cancel{2\times3\times6}\ 36}$$

$$\frac{}{36}$$

e. Read what you add for the top of the answer. (**Signal.**) *18 plus 24 plus 30.*
- Tell me what that equals. (**Pause.**) (**Signal.**) *72.*

- (Write to show:)

$$\frac{1}{2}\left(\frac{3 \times 6}{3 \times 6}\right) = \frac{18}{2 \times 3 \times 6} \ 36$$

$$\frac{2}{3}\left(\frac{2 \times 6}{2 \times 6}\right) = \frac{24}{2 \times 3 \times 6} \ 36$$

$$+\frac{5}{6}\left(\frac{2 \times 3}{2 \times 3}\right) = \frac{30}{2 \times 3 \times 6} \ 36$$

$$\frac{72}{36}$$

- What's the answer for the problem? (Signal.) *72 over 36.*

EXERCISE 5

Workcheck

a. We're going to check the answers. Exchange workbooks and get ready to check the answers. **(Pause.)**
- Put an **X** next to each item you got wrong.
- (Read the answers for all rows. See ***Answer Key.***)
- Return workbooks.

b. Now we're going to figure out the number of points you've earned for this lesson.
- (Point to the posted information.)

Worksheet Items	Errors	Points
	0–2	10
	3	7
	4	5
	5	3
	6	1
	7 or more	0

- Count the number of items you got wrong. Figure out the number of points you earned and write the number in the "Items" box.

- (Observe students and give feedback.)

c. (Tell the group how many points they earned for the lesson.) Write that number in the "Hard Work" box; then figure out the total for today's lesson.

d. Turn to the Point Summary Charts. Write the points in the box for Lesson 5. ✔

e. Total your points for Lessons 1 through 5 and write the total number on the chart.
- (Observe students and give feedback.)

f. Everybody, find the Five-Lesson Point Graph on page 120. ✔
- (Help the students plot their five-lesson scores on the graph.)

Lesson 5

Items + Hard Work = TOTAL

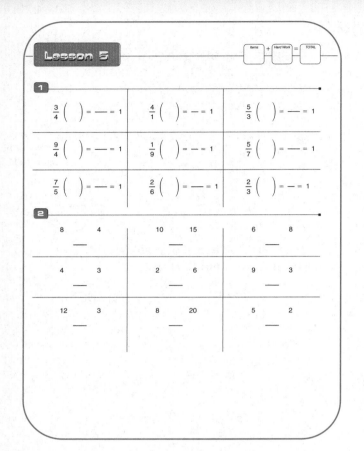

1

$\frac{3}{4}\left(\ \ \right) = \underline{\ \ } = 1$ $\frac{4}{1}\left(\ \ \right) = \underline{\ \ } = 1$ $\frac{5}{3}\left(\ \ \right) = \underline{\ \ } = 1$

$\frac{9}{4}\left(\ \ \right) = \underline{\ \ } = 1$ $\frac{1}{9}\left(\ \ \right) = \underline{\ \ } = 1$ $\frac{5}{7}\left(\ \ \right) = \underline{\ \ } = 1$

$\frac{7}{5}\left(\ \ \right) = \underline{\ \ } = 1$ $\frac{2}{6}\left(\ \ \right) = \underline{\ \ } = 1$ $\frac{2}{3}\left(\ \ \right) = \underline{\ \ } = 1$

2

8 4   10 15   6 8

4 3   2 6   9 3

12 3   8 20   5 2

Point Summary Charts

1.

Lesson	1	2	3	4	5	Total
Points						

2.

Lesson	6	7	8	9	10	Total
Points						

3.

Lesson	11	12	13	14	15	Total
Points						

4.

Lesson	16	17	18	19	20	Total
Points						

5.

Lesson	21	22	23	24	25	Total
Points						

6.

Lesson	26	27	28	29	30	Total
Points						

7.

Lesson	31	32	33	34	35	Total
Points						

8.

Lesson	36	37	38	39	40	Total
Points						

9.

Lesson	41	42	43	44	44 R	45	Total
Points							

10.

Lesson	46	47	48	49	49 R	50	Total
Points							

11.

Lesson	51	52	53	54	55	Total
Points						

12.

Lesson	56	56 R	57	58	59	60	Total
Points							

13.

Lesson	61	62	63	63 R	64	65	Total
Points							

14.

Lesson	66	67	68	69	70	Total
Points						
REV	70		71		72	

Daily Points

Daily points will be awarded by the teacher as follows:

1. **Oral Work** 0–3 group points for working hard and answering on signal. Everyone in the group will receive the same number of points for oral work.

2. **Worksheet Items**

Errors	Points
0–2	10
3	7
4	5
5	3
6	1
7 or more	0

A grade: The average of five-lesson totals is at least 50 points.
B grade: The average of five-lesson totals is 40–49 points.
C grade: The average of five-lesson totals is 30–39 points.
An average of five-lesson totals of less than 30 points is a failing grade for this course.

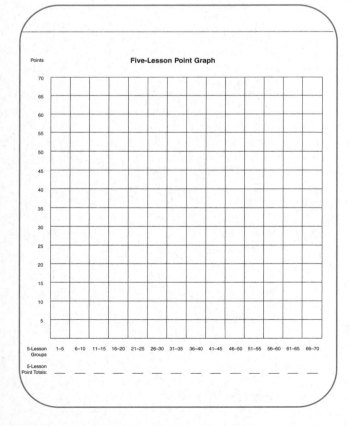

Five-Lesson Point Graph

Points

70 65 60 55 50 45 40 35 30 25 20 15 10 5

5-Lesson Groups: 1–5 6–10 11–15 16–20 21–25 26–30 31–35 36–40 41–45 46–50 51–55 56–60 61–65 66–70

5-Lesson Point Totals:

Changing by Multiplying

a.   (Write on the board:) $\dfrac{5}{3}\left(\right)=\dfrac{1}{4}$

b.   What does the problem say?(Signal)
"Five thirds times some fraction equals one fourth."

c.   You have to figure out that fraction. What do I write first? (Signal)
"Three fifths."

(Write:) $\dfrac{5}{3}\left(\dfrac{3}{5}\right)=\dfrac{1}{4}$

d.   What do I write next? (Signal)
"Times one fourth."

(Write:) $\dfrac{5}{3}\left(\dfrac{3}{5}\times\dfrac{1}{4}\right)=\dfrac{1}{4}$

e.   Look inside the bracket. When you multiply, what is on the top? (Signal)
"Three."

(Write:) $\dfrac{5}{3}\left(\dfrac{\cancel{3}\;^{3}}{5}\times\dfrac{\cancel{1}}{4}\right)=\dfrac{1}{4}$

f.   What is on the bottom? (Signal)
"Twenty."

(Write:) $\dfrac{5}{3}\left(\dfrac{\cancel{3}\;^{3}}{\underset{20}{\cancel{5}}}\times\dfrac{\cancel{1}}{4}\right)=\dfrac{1}{4}$

g.   We're done. Five thirds times some fraction equals one fourth.
What is that fraction? (Signal)
"Three twentieths."

Changing by Multiplying - Proof

a.   (Write on the board:) $\dfrac{2}{1}\left(\right)=\dfrac{8}{1}$

b. You know the answer to this problem. Two times how many equals eight? (Signal)
"Four."

c. You know the answer has to be four.
Let's work the problem the new way and see if we get a fraction that is equal to four.
What does the problem say? (Signal)
"Two over one times some fraction equals eight over one."

d. To figure out that fraction, what do I write first? (Signal)
"One half."

(Write:) $\dfrac{2}{1}\left(\dfrac{1}{2}\qquad\right)=\dfrac{8}{1}$

e. What do I write next? (Signal)
"Times eight over one."

(Write:) $\dfrac{2}{1}\left(\dfrac{1}{2}\times\dfrac{8}{1}\right)=\dfrac{8}{1}$

f. When you multiply inside the brackets, what is on the top? (Signal)
"Eight."

(Write:) $\dfrac{2}{1}\left(\dfrac{\overset{8}{\cancel{1}}}{2}\times\dfrac{\cancel{8}}{1}\right)=\dfrac{8}{1}$

g. What is on the bottom? (Signal)
"Two."

(Write:) $\dfrac{2}{1}\left(\dfrac{\overset{8}{\cancel{1}}}{\underset{2}{\cancel{2}}}\times\dfrac{\cancel{8}}{\cancel{1}}\right)=\dfrac{8}{1}$

h. Two over one times some fraction equals eight over one.
What is that fraction? (Signal)
"Eight over two."

i. How many times bigger is the top of that fraction than the bottom? (Signal)
"Four."

j. So what number does eight over two equal? (Signal)
"Four."

k. The answer is right. We know that two times four equals eight. And that is the answer we got.

---

a. (Write on the board:) $\dfrac{3}{1}\left(\qquad\right)=\dfrac{9}{1}$

You know the answer to this problem. Three times how many equals nine? (Signal)
"Three."

b. You know the answer has to be three.
Let's work the problem the new way and see if we get a fraction that is equal to three.
What does the problem say? (Signal)
"Three over one times some fraction equals nine over one."

c. To figure out that fraction, what do I write first? (Signal)
   "One over three."

   (Write:) $\dfrac{3}{1}\left(\dfrac{1}{3}\qquad\right)=\dfrac{9}{1}$

d. What do I write next? (Signal)
   "Times nine over one."

   (Write:) $\dfrac{3}{1}\left(\dfrac{1}{3}\times\dfrac{9}{1}\right)=\dfrac{9}{1}$

e. When you multiply inside the brackets, what is on the top? (Signal)
   "Nine."

   (Write:) $\dfrac{3}{1}\left(\dfrac{\cancel{1}}{3}\times\dfrac{\overset{9}{\cancel{9}}}{1}\right)=\dfrac{9}{1}$

f. What is on the bottom? (Signal)
   "Three."

   (Write:) $\dfrac{3}{1}\left(\dfrac{\cancel{1}}{\underset{3}{\cancel{3}}}\overset{9}{\times}\dfrac{\cancel{9}}{\cancel{1}}\right)=\dfrac{9}{1}$

g. Three over one times some fraction equals nine over one.
   What is that fraction? (Signal)
   "Nine over three."

h. The top of nine over three is how many times bigger than the bottom? (Signal)
   "Three."

i. So what number does nine over three equal? (Signal)
   "Three."

j. The answer is right. We know that three times three equals nine.
   And that is the answer we got.

Changing by Multiplying - Reverse

a. (Write on the board:) $\dfrac{5}{2}=\left(\qquad\right)\dfrac{1}{4}$

b. The new way for changing numbers works both directions.
   The arrow always shows you which way to work.
   In this problem, you start with one fourth.
   Read this problem by following the arrow. (Signal)
   "One fourth times some fraction equals five halves."
   (Repeat until firm.)

c. You have to figure out that fraction. What do I write first to change one fourth into one?
   (Signal)
   "Four over one."

   (Write:) $\dfrac{5}{2}=\left(\dfrac{4}{1}\right)\dfrac{1}{4}$

d. What does the side with the bracket equal? (Signal)
   "One."

e. One times what fraction equals five halves? (Signal)
   "Five halves."

   (Write:) $\dfrac{5}{2} = \left(\dfrac{5}{2} \times \dfrac{4}{1}\right) \dfrac{1}{4}$

f. Look inside the brackets. When you multiply, what is on the top? (Signal)
   "Twenty."

   (Write:) $\dfrac{5}{2} = \left(\dfrac{\cancel{5}}{2} \overset{20}{\times} \dfrac{\cancel{4}}{1}\right) \dfrac{1}{4}$

g. What is on the bottom? (Signal)
   "Two."

   (Write:) $\dfrac{5}{2} = \left(\dfrac{\cancel{5}}{\cancel{2}\,2} \overset{20}{\times} \dfrac{4}{\cancel{1}}\right) \dfrac{1}{4}$

h. We're done. One fourth times some fraction equals five halves.
   What is that fraction?(Signal)
   "Twenty halves."

Changing by Multiplying

a. Turn to Worksheet 3 . Copy this problem in Part A.

   (Write on the board:) $\dfrac{4}{1} = \left(\right)\dfrac{7}{6}$

   To tell what the problem says, start with seven sixths and follow the arrow.
   What does the problem say? (Signal)
   "Seven sixths times some fraction equals four over one."
   (Repeat until firm.)

b. You have to figure out the fraction. First you have to change seven sixths into one.
   Write the fraction that changes seven sixths into one. Write it next to the seven sixths. (Pause)
   How many do you have on the side with the bracket? (Signal)
   "One."

c. One times how many equals four over one? (Signal)
   "Four over one."

d. What are you going to write? (Signal)
   "Times four over one."

e. Write it. (Pause)
   Multiply and figure out the fraction inside the bracket. (Pause)
   Seven sixths times some fraction equals four over one. What is that fraction? (Signal)
   "Twenty-four sevenths."

a. Copy this problem.

(Write on the board:) $\frac{1}{3} = \left(\phantom{\xleftarrow{\hspace{1.5cm}}}\right)\frac{4}{5}$

Read the problem. Start on four fifths and follow the arrow. (Signal)
"Four fifths times some fraction equals one third."

b. You have to figure out the fraction. First you have to change four fifths into one.
Write the fraction that changes four fifths into one. Write it next to the four fifths. (Pause)
How many do you have on the side with the bracket? (Signal)
"One."

c. One times how many equals one third? (Signal)
"One third."

d. What are you going to write? (Signal)
"Times one third."

e. Write it. (Pause)
Multiply and figure out the fraction inside the brackets. (Pause)
Four fifths times some fraction equals one third. What is that fraction? (Signal)
"Five twelfths."

a. What does the next problem say? (Signal)
*"Three fourths times some fraction
equals two fifths."*

$\frac{2}{5} = \left(\phantom{\xleftarrow{\hspace{1.2cm}}}\right)\frac{3}{4}$

b. What do you change three fourths into first? (Signal)
"One."

c. Do it. (Pause)
How many do you have on the side with the brackets? (Signal)
"One."

d. What do you write next? (Signal)
"Times two fifths."

e. Do it. Then figure out the fraction in the brackets. (Pause)
Three fourths times some fraction equals two fifths. What is that fraction? (Signal)
"Eight fifteenths."

a. Go across. What does the next
problem say? (Signal)
*"Five over one times some fraction
equals two thirds."*

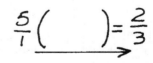

$\frac{5}{1}\left(\phantom{\xrightarrow{\hspace{1.2cm}}}\right) = \frac{2}{3}$

b. What do you change five over one into first? (Signal)
"One."

c. Do it. (Pause)
How many do you have on the side with the brackets? (Signal)
"One."

d. What do you write next? (Signal)
   "Times two thirds."

e. Do it. Then figure out the fraction in the brackets. (Pause)
   Five over one times some fraction equals two thirds. What is that fraction? (Signal)
   "Two fifteenths."

f. Finish the rest of the problems in Part A. Watch which way the arrow goes.

Simple Ratios

a. Touch the first problem in Part B.
   You have to find the missing numbers. To do that, you have to figure
   out the fraction of one. First draw
   the arrows. Make both arrows
   point to the side with the empty box.
   (Pause, Check)

$$\frac{5}{4} \quad \frac{()}{()} = \quad \frac{\Box}{16}$$

b. Where do you work first in that problem, on the top or the bottom? (Signal)
   "On the bottom."

c. Follow the arrow and figure out what you multiply by. (Pause)
   What do you multiply by on the bottom? (Signal)
   "Four."

d. Write that number in the bracket. (Pause)
   What do you write in the bracket on the top? (Signal)
   "Four."

e. Write it. (Pause)
   What is the fraction of one that you multiply five fourths by? (Signal)
   "Four fourths."

f. Follow the arrow and write the missing number. (Pause)
   What is the missing number? (Signal)
   "Twenty."

a. Touch the next problem. Draw the
   arrows. Make them point to the side
   with the empty box. (Pause)
   Where do you work first in that
   problem? (Signal)
   "On the top."

$$\frac{21}{\Box} \quad \frac{()}{()} = \quad \frac{7}{5}$$

b. Follow the arrow and figure out what you multiply by. (Pause)
   What do you multiply by on the top? (Signal)
   "Three."

c. Write that number in the brackets. Then fill in the other bracket. (Pause)
   What is the fraction of one that you multiply seven fifths by? (Signal)
   "Three thirds."

d. Follow the arrow and write the missing number. (Pause)
   What is the missing number? (Signal)
   "Fifteen."

e. Work the rest of the problems in Part B. Draw the arrows so they point to the side with
   the empty box. Then figure out the fraction of one and fill in the empty box.

Substitution

a. Look at the first problem in Part C.
What does the problem say? (Signal)
"Five times M."

$$5 \times M =$$

b. What's another way of writing five times M? (Signal)
"Five M."

c. Write that. (Pause)
Go down.
What does the next problem say? (Signal)
"Eight times R."

$$8 \times R =$$

d. What's another way of writing eight times R? (Signal)
"Eight R."

e. Write that. (Pause)
What does the next problem say? (Signal)
"Eight R."

$$8R =$$

f. Think about it. What's the other way of writing eight R? (Signal)
"Eight times R."
(To correct:) Eight times R. That's the other way of writing it. One way is eight R.
The other way is eight times R.

g. Write eight times R. (Pause)
What does the next problem say? (Signal)
"Eighteen C."

$$18C =$$

h. What's the other way of writing eighteen C? (Signal)
"Eighteen times C."

i. Write it. (Pause)
Work the rest of the problems in Part C. Write each problem the other way.

Workcheck

a. Exchange workbooks and get ready to check the answers. (Pause)
Put an X next to any problems that the person misses.
(Read the entire problem with the answer.)

b. Figure out how many problems the person missed.
Then write the number of errors at the top of the worksheet. (Pause)
Return the workbooks.

c. Everybody turn to your chart. Write the number of errors on your chart.
Then figure out how many points you get and write that on your chart. (Pause)
Under group points, everybody gets _____ points. (Pause)
Add up your points for today.

Worshsheet 3   errors: _____

A.

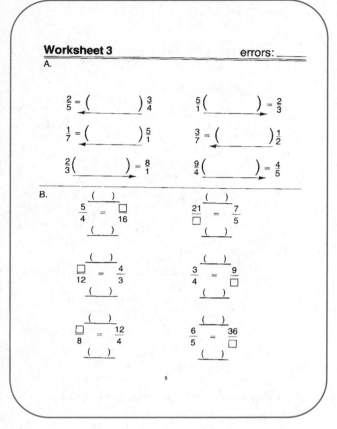

$\frac{2}{5} = ($ _____ $) \frac{3}{4}$ $\frac{5}{1} ($ _____ $) = \frac{2}{3}$

$\frac{1}{7} = ($ _____ $) \frac{5}{1}$ $\frac{3}{7} = ($ _____ $) \frac{1}{2}$

$\frac{2}{3} ($ _____ $) = \frac{8}{1}$ $\frac{9}{4} ($ _____ $) = \frac{4}{5}$

B.

$\frac{(\quad)}{5}{4} = \frac{\square}{16}$ $\frac{21}{\square} = \frac{7}{5}$

$\frac{\square}{12} = \frac{4}{3}$ $\frac{3}{4} = \frac{9}{\square}$

$\frac{\square}{8} = \frac{12}{4}$ $\frac{6}{5} = \frac{36}{\square}$

5

$5 \times M =$ $\frac{3}{5} \times B =$ $F \times D =$

$8 \times R =$ $12Y =$ $\frac{7}{9} T =$

$8R =$ $CB =$ $3R =$

$18C =$ $\frac{7}{6} \times F =$ $5 \times B =$

6

Questions and Answers

Should the modules be taught in a particular order?
Because the program's skill sequence is developmental and later modules build on skills presented in earlier modules, the first four modules of *Corrective Mathematics* must be presented in this order: *Addition, Subtraction, Multiplication,* and *Division. Basic Fractions* can be presented after *Addition, Subtraction,* and *Multiplication. Fractions, Decimals, and Percents* builds on skills taught in *Basic Fractions.*

Should all students be taught all modules?
If students are deficient in the skills presented in any of the modules, you would present the modules in order. However, all students need not begin with *Addition.* For example, a student who is proficient in addition and subtraction would begin with the *Multiplication* module and then go to *Division* or *Basic Fractions.*

How can I determine which modules are appropriate for my students?
The Comprehensive Placement Test will determine the module in which the students should begin the *Corrective Mathematics* series and the specific lesson on which the students should start. The test will also identify those students who are too advanced for any of the *Corrective Mathematics* modules as well as those students who are too low for any module in the series.

What materials are required for *Corrective Mathematics*?
Each module consists of a Teacher's Presentation Book, an Answer Key booklet, and one Workbook for each student. Optional **Exam***View* software allows you to generate customized worksheets for practicing facts, computation, and test-taking formats.

How much instructional time does *Corrective Mathematics* require?
Each lesson will take between 25 and 45 minutes depending on the size of the group and the students' proficiency in reading story problems.

What are the advantages of the planned presentations?
The program provides a complete script of each lesson's activities. The scripts have been thoroughly tested to ensure that they communicate concepts clearly and are easily understood by students. For you, scripted lessons eliminate time-consuming lesson planning, which means that all your energy can be focused on teaching. For students, scripted lessons provide consistent lesson structure that eliminates anxious guessing about what is expected of them.

Do students receive adequate practice and review on skills they are taught?
Review is a fundamental part of every *Corrective Mathematics* lesson.

When a skill is first introduced, you provide step-by-step guidance as students work several problems. In later lessons, you give less guidance as skills are reviewed and expanded until students are working problems by themselves. All these activities incorporate review, but problems that are specifically for review appear in independent work throughout each module. In addition to practice found on worksheets, blackline masters for *Addition, Subtraction, Multiplication,* and *Division* provide ongoing, cumulative practice.

Do the students work independently?
During much of the lesson, you are guiding the lesson, ensuring that the students comprehend new concepts and that individual needs are met directly and effectively. You present exercises, listen to student responses, and correct errors immediately. Serious error patterns don't have a chance to develop. Students work independently only after you have established that they can successfully complete the activities.

What if I can't complete a lesson in the time allotted?

Your *primary* goal should be to teach responsively. At the conclusion of any exercise, each student should be *firm*—able to respond to all parts without making mistakes. Often you will have to repeat tasks to make sure that students are firm. If your initial criterion for a task is strict, the group will have less difficulty with similar tasks in subsequent lessons.

If you find that you cannot average at least a lesson a day after you have become familiar with the programs, there is a good chance your pacing is too slow. Make quick pacing your number one goal for yourself for the next several lessons. Read the lesson ahead of time so you are familiar with the content and teaching procedures. Practice the script aloud. Continue practicing until you can present each exercise at a relatively rapid rate.

What kind of standardized tests can I use with *Corrective Mathematics*?

The standardized test you use should correspond to the content of the modules you're teaching.

When possible, remedial students should be tested using a test that includes 4th- or 5th-grade math content. This is because remedial students are likely to make impressive gains without their gains being reflected by an on-level test. Tenth graders, for instance, who improve from a 4th- to a 6th-grade level will not show these gains on a 10th-grade test because a 10th-grade test measures the content of the 10th-grade curriculum.

Notes

Notes

Notes

Notes

Notes

Notes

Notes

Notes

Notes

Notes

Notes

Notes

Notes

Notes